COLLINS GEM GUIDES

STEAM
TRAINS

General Editor

Derek Avery

COLLINS
London and Glasgow

First published 1987
Wm Collins Sons & Co Ltd
Reprint 10 9 8 7 6 5 4 3 2 1 0
© Chevprime Ltd 1987

Produced by Chevprime Ltd
147 Cleveland Street
London W1

ISBN 0 00 458852 5

Artwork by R.P. Gossop & Co
Filmset by Computerised Typesetting
Services Ltd
Printed in Great Britain by Collins,
Glasgow

Contents

LNER Class A4 Pacific No 4498 Sir Nigel Gresley

Introduction

The advantages to be gained by running wheeled vehicles, especially those carrying heavy loads, on relatively smooth rails rather than rough and uneven ground, have been appreciated for many centuries. As early as 1550, illustrations appeared of wagonways used in German mines, and over the next 200 years their use became common in mines all over Europe. In Britain, especially, they were used to ferry coal from the mines to nearby rivers and, later, to the canals.

For many years only wooden rails were used, and the wheels of the wagons had grooved or flanged rims for guidance. Later, iron plating was added to prolong the life of the rails, and towards the end of the eighteenth century cast-iron plates, usually laid on stone blocks and formed with flanges to guide plain wheels, became more common.

At the same time, other operators began to experiment with iron rails, rather than plates, which were intended for use with flanged wheels. The next step was the introduction of wrought iron, which enabled much longer rails to be used, and in 1820 a system of rolling lengths of wrought iron of uniform cross-section was patented. Ultimately, the modern forms of railway track were evolved.

Where navigable rivers did not exist, the construction of canals was an expensive business, and by the beginning of the nineteenth century there were numerous schemes for long-distance railways. In

1801 a significant step was taken when the Surrey Iron Railway was authorized by Act of Parliament to carry public traffic over the 14.5km (9mls) between Croydon and the River Thames at Wandsworth, and in 1803 it opened as the first officially sanctioned public railway.

However, as long as the wagons were drawn by horses there were practical limits on the weight and speed of traffic that railways could carry. The steam engines that were becoming increasingly common by the end of the eighteenth century seemed to offer a promising source of power and, as early as 1769, Nicolas Cugnot had built a steam carriage in Paris, only to be imprisoned for his pains. By the time the Surrey Iron Railway was opened in 1803, an English engineer, Richard Trevithick, had produced his first steam-propelled vehicle for use on the roads.

Trevithick was the son of a mine engineer in Cornwall, and in 1801 he built a successful steam carriage which incorporated a return flue to heat the water in the boiler. A second steam carriage was followed by a locomotive designed to run on the plateway between the Penydaren ironworks, in South Wales, and a local canal. On 21 February 1804 Trevithick's locomotive hauled ten tons of iron, augmented by a number of passengers, the length of the 16.1km (10mls) plateway, though only at the cost of heavy damage to the iron plates.

This pioneer locomotive employed a single horizontal cylinder, with a large flywheel, and the wheels were driven through a system of gears, while his *Catch-me-who-can* of 1808 used a vertical cylinder to drive the wheels by means of connecting rods.

In 1805 Trevithick built another engine for the Wylam colliery. This engine, like the Penydaren model, proved too heavy for the plateway, but it inspired a number of local engineers to build their own experimental locomotives. The most important of these engineers was George Stephenson.

Although barely literate, Stephenson was both a mechanical genius and a visionary, who not only perfected the basic pattern on which all steam locomotives were based, but also foresaw the creation of a national railway network. Each of Stephenson's locomotives embodied further improvements on Trevithick's original pattern: his first, the *Blücher*, of 1814, had flanged wheels to run on rails rather than plates, and in subsequent engines he perfected a direct drive from the cylinders via connecting rods to the driving wheels. When he became involved in the planning of the Stockton and Darlington Railway, Stephenson adopted wrought-iron I-section rails, mounted in chairs on the stone blocks to provide continuity in the joints, and his first locomotive for the new railway, the *Locomotion*, used rods rather than chains to connect the two pairs of wheels.

The opening of the Stockton and Darlington Railway on 27 September 1825 was an historic occasion, marking the first use of steam power on a public railway, but the locomotives were still prone to boiler explosions and broken wheels. By this time George Stephenson had become the acknowledged expert on railways and locomotives, and he was invited to advise on the construction and operation of a projected railway between Liverpool and Manchester.

A series of trials was held at Rainhill in October 1829 and the undoubted star of the contest was the *Rocket,* built by the firm which George Stephenson had founded and of which his son Robert was the head. The essential features of the *Rocket,* which were to endure throughout the development of the steam locomotive, were the multitube boiler and the blast pipe. Hot gases from the fire passed through the firetubes in the boiler, heating the water to produce steam. The steam was fed to the cylinders, where, by acting on the pistons, it drove the wheels and was then exhausted through a blast pipe in the chimney to create the draught on the fire.

By the time the Liverpool and Manchester Railway was ready to begin operations in September 1830, news of the new steam railways was creating widespread interest. Across the Atlantic, where settlement of the fertile river valleys in the interior of the United States was getting under way, there was a desperate need for improved communications.

The response of the east-coast cities, once New York had secured the first water route to the Great Lakes, was to seek their own means of communications, and with the mountain ranges forming a formidable obstacle to new canals, a number of them

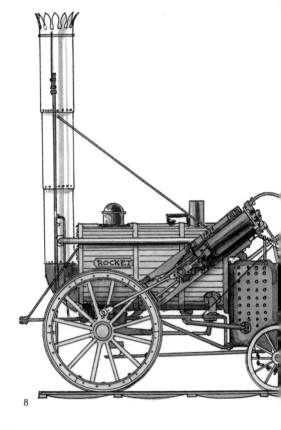

8

THE ROCKET

Country of Origin: UK
Railway: Liverpool & Manchester Railway
Date: 1827
Length Overall: 6.55m (21ft 6in)
Total Weight: 4.545kg (10,000lb)
Cylinders: 2 203 × 419mm (8 × 16.5in)
Driving Wheels: 1.435m (4ft 8.5in)

turned to railways as a possible solution.

First in the race was Baltimore, and in February 1828 the Maryland state legislature chartered the Baltimore and Ohio Railroad, an ambitious scheme for a 611.8km (380mls) railway that would connect with the Ohio River at Wheeling. Work was begun on 4 July 1829, and by the following year horses were hauling rail cars over the first 20.9km (13mls) of track.

Already, a steam locomotive had been tested in the United States: the Delaware and Hudson Canal company had sent Horatio Allen to observe the Rainhill trials, and he had ordered four locomotives, one from Robert Stephenson and the rest from the Stourbridge firm of Foster & Rastrick. It was one of the latter, the *Stourbridge Lion,* which on 9 August 1829 made the first steam locomotive trip in America, and a year later the *Tom Thumb,* built by one of the Baltimore and Ohio shareholders, Peter Cooper, was tested on the B&O's track between Baltimore and Ellicott's Mills.

On 28 August *Tom Thumb* pulled a coach carrying 36 passengers at speeds of up to 29km/h (18mph). The railroad offered prizes for the best locomotives to be entered in a competition held on 1 June 1831. The only locomotive able to meet the conditions of the competition was the *York,* built by Phineas Davis, and as a result the Baltimore and Ohio ordered 20 further examples of Davis's 'grasshopper' engines. The first of these was named *Atlantic,* and several of the class served the railroad for over 50 years.

By this time, other cities had followed Baltimore's lead, and railroads were being built westwards from Boston, Philadelphia, Richmond, Charleston and Savannah. Within a few years, others were started to connect the inland cities with the lakes, rivers and seas that still formed the main long-distance transport routes, and new firms were building locomotives to operate them. By the middle of the nineteenth century the United States would have the biggest rail network in the world, and the railways would go on to transform the Republic, but in the meantime the more industrialized nations of Europe were able to make better progress with the development of the railways.

The first railway in France was opened between Andrezieux and St Etienne in 1828, though steam traction was not introduced until 1832 on a new line from St Etienne to Lyons. New lines followed in Germany and Belgium in 1835, and by the end of the decade steam railways were also in operation in Ireland, Austria, the Netherlands and Italy. Other countries followed suit during the 1840s, and while these usually relied on locomotives built by Stephenson or other English constructors to begin with, national characteristics soon became apparent as indigenous designs were produced.

One consequence of the initial use of Stephenson locomotives, however, was the widespread adoption of Stephenson's 'standard' gauge, or distance between the rails, of 143.5cm (4ft 8.5in). This was selected in the first place for no better reason than it happened to be the gauge used on the mine railway where Stephenson's first experiments were carried out, but ultimately the benefits of uniformity outweighed the drawbacks of the restricted width, and only Russia, Finland, Spain and Portugal chose different gauges. Consequently, it was soon possible to run international trains through most of Europe.

Another characteristic of the continental railways was the large measure of government control that was exercised over their location. In the United States and Britain many competing lines were built, and it was many years before even the gauge was standardized on a national basis. Elsewhere in Europe, on the other hand, the tendency was for the national governments to license private companies to build along selected routes, or to undertake the construction themselves, thus avoiding a good deal of the wasteful competition that was to mar the development of the British and American systems.

The success of the Liverpool and Manchester venture sparked off almost unbounded enthusiasm for new lines in Britain, and within a few years new lines were being planned, built and opened all over the country.

In 1837 the Grand Junction Railway was opened between Warrington and Birmingham to complete the first trunk route between the latter city and Liverpool and Manchester. And while George Stephenson was engaged on the Grand Junction, his son, Robert, was at work on a route from Birmingham to London.

By the end of the nineteenth century, the majority of the small lines that had appeared early in the development of the railway system in Britain had been consolidated into a number of large companies. All of these developed their own characteristic styles, which were reflected in the architecture of their stations, the pattern of their services and, most visibly, in the brightly painted locomotives.

British express services were easily the fastest in the world during the 1880s, though trains were relatively light and sustained speeds of 64.4-80.5km/h (40-50mph) rather than really high maximum speeds were the rule. The introduction of bogie passenger carriages during the 1870s enabled a new level of comfort to be provided and, together with the adoption of continuous brakes, block signalling and other safety measures, permitted considerably higher speeds. Improved track also encouraged faster running, and towards the end of the 1880s there were the first signs of an acceleration in scheduled services.

The premier long-distance route was that from London to Edinburgh. On 21 August 1889, the east-coast lines pushed the speed to an average of 97.6km/h (60.6mph) using one of the Great Northern's Stirling 243.8cm (8ft) singles between King's Cross and York, and North Eastern and North British 4-4-0s for the remainder of the journey. The following night, the west-coast companies replied with a time of only 8hrs 32mins for the 869.4km (540 mls) trip for a record average speed of 101.8km/h (63mph). The engines involved in this achievement were a three-cylinder compound 4-4-0 between Euston and Crewe and the Precedent class 2-4-0 *Hardwicke* from Crewe to Carlisle, followed by Caledonian Railway 4-4-0s for the rest of the run to Aberdeen.

Meanwhile, the development of railways in the United States had followed a radically different course from that in Britain. Despite some early set-backs they continued to spread, and by 1850 there were some 14,490km (9,000mls) of railway in operation. Another decade saw that total more than trebled, but the 1860s brought the Civil War and a temporary pause in new construction.

By the time the War ended in 1865, the United States Military Railroads (USMRR) was operating more than 400 locomotives and 6,000 cars, controlled over 3,220km (2,000mls) of track, and had been responsible for the repair of many bridges and sections of track that had been destroyed by enemy action.

The most significant wartime development, however, was the chartering of the first transcontinental railway. In July 1862 President Lincoln signed the act authorizing the construction of the Pacific railroad, which was to be built between the banks of the Missouri (at the site which became the city of Omaha, Nebraska), and Sacramento, California. The final junction of the two sets of track was made at Promontory, Utah, on 10 May 1869. Golden spikes were driven to join the actual rails, and representative locomotives from each railroad steamed forward to touch pilots in a symbolic meeting of east and west.

The completion of the first transcontinental line marked the start of a period of unparalleled expansion of the American rail network. New transcontinental lines were built, as the Southern Pacific and Santa Fe railroads crossed the southern territories, and the Northern Pacific, Great Northern, Burlington and Milwaukee railroads spanned the northwest. Connecting lines were built in all directions, and by the end of the century there was a network of 310,730km (193,000mls) of railroad.

In Britain by 1902, daily services were run between London and Birmingham at 89.4km/h (55.5mph), and in 1903 the fastest service on the run to Bristol was scheduled at just under 96.6km/h (60mph). In 1904 the *City of Truro* inaugurated the Cornish Riviera Express, the longest non-stop run in the world, which averaged 89.4km/h (55.5mph) for the 395.3km (245.5mls) journey.

The growing weight of these fast services called for more powerful locomotives, and the logical step was to add a third pair of driving wheels. This solution was adopted by most of the main-line companies before the First World War, most successfully on the Great Western in the form of the series of 4-6-0s designed by George Churchward. His two-cylinder Saint and four-cylinder Star classes were outstanding engines, and after his retirement in 1921 the Star type was developed into the famous Castle class.

The first of the Castles, *Caerphilly Castle,* appeared in 1923, and the type proved so successful that modified versions were still being built in 1950. The four-cylinder 4-6-0s of the Lord Nelson class, which were provided to deal with the heaviest expresses on the Southern Railway, were designed after studies of the Castle class. Churchward's influence also led to the Stanier-designed Black Five 4-6-0s, of which no fewer than 842 were built between 1934 and 1951, and which proved capable of virtually any type of work.

Meanwhile, the trend in the biggest passenger engines had been towards the Pacific type, whose pair of rear carrying wheels allowed a bigger firebox to be used.

In 1928 production of the A3 Pacifics began and the new engines were spectacularly successful. In March 1935, on a special trial run between King's Cross and Newcastle-upon-Tyne, the A3 *Papyrus* covered well over half the 864.6km (537mls) round trip at 128.8km/h (80mph), reaching a maximum speed of 173.9km/h (108mph) and recording an average of 112.3km/h (69.8mph) for the return trip from Newcastle. The first of the new A4 Pacific designs, *Silver Link,* made its public debut on a special trial in September 1935, and more records were broken, with a top speed of 181.1km/h (112.5mph) being recorded.

In 1933, the LMSR introduced the new Princess class Pacifics for the Royal Scot service between London and Glasgow and, following the introduction of the streamlined Silver Jubilee train, the company set about producing its own streamlined Pacifics. The first of the new engines were built for a new service inaugurated in 1937 and named the Coronation Scot, which was scheduled to cover the 645.6km (401 miles) between London and Glasgow in 6.5 hours.

By this time, the London and North Eastern had introduced a six-hour service between London and Edinburgh, the Coronation, which involved speeds of 161km/h (100mph) on many occasions, and in 1938, under the pretext of carrying out braking trials, an all-out attempt was made at a new speed record. The engine was the A4 Pacific *Mallard*, and on 3 July a speed of 202.9km/h (126mph) was reached with the Silver Jubilee train and a special dynamometer car to record the performance. The record was established only at the cost of severe overheating, and the following year the Second World War intervened to put a stop to further attempts at increased.speeds on the Scottish services.

In 1937 Oliver Bulleid became chief mechanical engineer on the Southern Railway, which had for some years been engaged in electrifying sections of its main line. Bulleid's first move was to improve many members of the existing Lord Nelson, King Arthur and Schools classes by the addition of Lemaitre multiple blast pipes. In his original designs, Bulleid showed a tendency to innovation on a comprehensive scale. The most obvious feature of his Merchant Navy class Pacifics, which first appeared in

1941, was the 'air-smoothed' casing, but along with the striking exterior came a wealth of novel details. The valve gear was enclosed in an oil bath, the firebox and high-pressure boiler, which tapered underneath to accommodate the inside cylinder, were of welded steel, and the wheels were an adaption of the American 'Boxpok' type, while minor features included electric lighting and steampowered firedoors.

In 1948 the government nationalized the railway companies, and the new national company became known as British Railways. The last steam engine built for British Railways, the appropriately named *Evening Star*, was a member of the Class 9 2-10-0 heavy freight series. Although designed for maximum power, the Class 9 was also intended for use on mixed services, and in the event proved so versatile that it was capable of speeds of 144.9km/h (90mph), one example being used in an emergency to haul the Flying Scotsman.

Ten years after the announcement of the modernization plan, on 11 November 1965, the last regular steam-hauled passenger train left Paddington, and three years later the last regular goods services to be operated by steam came to an end. In the meantime, the plan entitled *The Reshaping of British Railways* had been published in 1962, and as a consequence the route mileage of British Railways was reduced from over 27,370km (17,000 miles) in the year of publication to under 19,320km (12,000 miles) by 1970, while passenger stations were reduced from 743 to

299 over the same period.

State ownership of railways began much earlier on the European mainland than in Britain. Alongside the principal companies in France, – for example the Nord, Est, Midi, Oest, Paris-Orléans (PO) and Paris-Lyons-Mediterranée (PLM), which had been organized by the government to radiate from Paris – in 1878 the état, or state system, was formed from a group of small companies in the west of the country.

The result was to create a competitor for the Paris-Orléans on the route to Bordeaux, while the Midi's control of the routes to Spain meant that the PO's services were in rivalry with those of the other connecting line, the PLM. With this stimulus, the PO built up the fastest trains in the country in the late nineteenth century, and in 1907, for its difficult main line to Toulouse, it introduced the first engines of the Pacific type in Europe.

These were four-cylinder de Glehn compounds, and a second series with superheaters was followed by a third with bigger driving wheels for the higher-speed services on the Bordeaux line. The compound system developed by Alfred de Glehn, and his partner Gaston du Bousquet, used a pair of high-pressure cylinders outside to drive the second pair of coupled wheels, and a low-pressure pair inside acting on the leading axle. The system was used widely in France and elsewhere in Europe, though in Britain, where George Churchward tested some French compound Atlantics, the additional complication of compounds never found wide acceptance, and the Pacifics introduced on the PO influenced other railways to follow suit.

Among the most prestigious of the French services were the Nord boat trains that formed the connection between Paris and Calais or Boulogne. In 1910 du Bousquet had been working on a 4-8-4 design for the Nord, but his death put an end to the development and the company was forced to adopt Pacifics of a type developed by de Glehn for the Alsace-Lorraine railway.

Previously, du Bousquet had designed for the Nord company a 4-6-0 with relatively small wheels and enlarged steam passages to give the necessary higher piston speeds. After the First World War, the Nord planned a new class of 'Super-Pacifics' using the larger steam passages developed for the 4-6-0. The first example had been designed by George Asselin in 1914, only for their production to be delayed by the First World War, but after their introduction in 1923 they proved capable of extremely heavy work. The last batch, the Collin 'Super-Pacifics' introduced in 1931, were able to maintain 96.6km/h (60mph) schedules with the 508 tonne (500 ton) boat trains between Paris and the Channel ports.

While these engines were being built for the Nord, one of the greatest of all locomotive designers had started work in the research department of the Paris-Orléans company. This was André Chapelon, who concentrated his efforts on improving the circulation of the steam. To this end he introduced internal streamlining of the steam passages, and increased the temperature in the superheaters to enable super-heated steam to be fed to the low-pressure cylinders. At the same time he adapted a device originated by the Finnish engineer Kylala for dividing the steamjet from the blast pipe to give improved draught on the fire without restricting the flow of the exhaust steam from the cylinders.

The result of these improvements, when applied to a PO Pacific, was an increase in power of 50 per cent, along with more economical use of fuel. Once the details became known, other French railways either bought new or rebuilt PO locomotives that were being made redundant by electrification, or applied Chapelon principles to their own designs. By 1938, when the various companies were absorbed into the Societé National des Chemins de Fer (national railway company), Chapelon's influence was dominant, though it was some years before he succeeded to the office of engineer-in-chief.

In Germany, both state-owned and private railways had been built from the beginning, and the formation of the German railway federation in 1917 was followed by the gradual absorption of the private lines into the state systems. The dominant member of the federation was Prussia, and after the First World War the majority of the locomotives built for the new Reichsbahn (state railway) were Prussian types.

However, the south German states of Bavaria,

Baden and Württemberg had produced many distinctive designs, and the Bavarian railway had pioneered the use of 4-6-0 and Pacific types for express passenger trains. The Bavarian S3/6 class Pacific, introduced in 1908, was the only non-Prussian type to be built for the Reichsbahn after its formation. They were constructed by the firm of Maffei, and were used on the fastest German trains, including the famous Rheingold express along the Rhine valley.

Of course, the great German contribution to steam locomotive design was the superheating system developed by Wilhelm Schmidt in the late 1890s. The purpose of superheating was to raise the temperature of the steam well above that produced in the boiler so that after expanding in the cylinders it would still be hot enough to avoid the condensation that occurred otherwise.

Various attempts were made to achieve the necessary extra degree of heating, but it was Schmidt's firetube system that superseded all others. Steam from the boiler was collected in a header in the smokebox, then led through enlarged firetubes, or flues, by narrow pipes, which doubled back to a second compartment in the header, whence it was fed to the cylinders.

The Prussian state railways were among the first to adopt the new device, which enabled compound operation to be dispensed with. Another benefit was that the superheated steam was able to do more work than the ordinary saturated steam, so that boiler pressures could be reduced and larger cylinders used instead, leading to a considerable reduction in maintenance requirements.

The most famous Prussian product of this period was the P8 class 4-6-0, of which some 3,850 were built, 3,370 going to the Prussian state railway alone. They remained in service for many years, and after the First World War were used by several other countries which received them as part of the war reparations Germany was forced to make after the Armistice.

In the period between the wars, Richard Wagner was responsible for the new locomotive designs for the Reichsbahn, and among his products was the 01 class Pacific, which, along with the later 03, became a standard type. The 231 examples of the 01 series were the principal passenger express locomotives of the period, though the typical low pressures and two-cylinder simple machinery meant they were not the fastest of engines, although this was compensated for by their durability.

After the Second World War, both the name and many of the locomotives of the Deutsches Reichsbahn were taken over by the German Democratic Republic, and a number of 01s were rebuilt with bigger boilers, Boxpok wheels, Giesl ejectors and other modifications.

Another of Wagner's designs that remained at the prototype stage was the streamlined 05 class 4-6-4. The first of two examples was completed in March 1935, and one subsequently reached a speed of

199.6km/h (124mph) on level track, a performance which compares favourably with the *Mallard*'s downhill record of 202.9km/h (126mph).

Italy was another European country where the original railways were built by individual states, and where electrification began at an early stage. It was only in 1870 that the unification of Italy was achieved, and the old state systems continued to operate until after the First World War.

Perhaps the best known 'fact' about Italian railways is that Mussolini made the trains run on time, though this is actually as much a myth as might be expected. The credit actually belongs to Carlo Crova, who in the 1920s was responsible, as general manager of the new state system, for the old Adriatic, Mediterranean and Sicilian systems, and who succeeded in imposing order and punctuality on them: the Fascists happened to be handily placed at the time to take the credit.

Among the locomotives that have operated on Italian railways are some unusual designs. In 1900 the Plancher type, with the cab in front of the boiler, was built to make life easier for the crew in the narrow tunnels of the Adriatic main line, and in 1937 another cab-in-front design was produced by Attilio Franco, whose concern was with improving boiler efficiency. Franco's ideas were developed by Piero Crosti into a distinctive type of boiler which carried feed water tanks alongside the main boiler, and led the exhaust gases through these to chimneys at the sides of the boiler.

This boiler was used on a series of 83 modified locomotives of the 743 class, among other Italian types, and was used on 10 of the British BR9 standard type 2-10-0s. As with other innovations of this period, however, it appeared too late for a full evaluation of its worth, though the extra complication of construction and maintenance would probably outweigh the savings of 10 per cent in fuel, except where coal was in short supply.

All the railway systems discussed so far have been of standard gauges, at least on the main lines, but there are two areas of Europe where a different gauge was chosen. One of these is the Iberian peninsula, where Spanish and Portuguese railways use a gauge of 167.6cm (5ft 6in). Spanish railways were initially built by both the various states and by private concerns, using imported locomotives. After the First World War, however, most Spanish locomotives were built there, and in 1941 the railways were nationalized.

Conditions on Spanish railways are often similar to those in Austria, with long-distance routes and many mountain sections, and the 4-8-0 was adopted at an early stage. Subsequent designs have typically had eight coupled driving wheels, with two or four leading and trailing wheels. A distinctive example is the F2001 class 4-8-4, a big and powerful type first built in 1955 and used to operate heavy passenger services.

The other European broad-gauge railway system is

at the opposite end of the continent, where Finnish and Russian railways are built to the 152.4cm (5ft) gauge. Finland has only about 4,830km (3,000mls) of route, and a correspondingly small number of locomotives, though steam locomotives continue in service. The two main classes are the Hr 1 Pacifics, for passenger traffic, and the Tr 1 2-8-2s for freight services.

Elsewhere in Scandinavia, the availability of hydroelectric power has led to electrification replacing steam, though in Sweden at one time numerous independent companies operated alongside the state system, and the variety of locomotive types was enormous.

India came to have one of the most varied railway systems in the world. Two 'standard' gauge networks were built, termed broad and metre gauge respectively, and subsequently many narrow-gauge lines were added – that is, narrower than the metre gauge. Currently, as many as 10 million passengers a day are carried on Indian trains, and while electrification is being carried out as rapidly as economic circumstances permit, much of the operation is still by steam.

Shortly after independence was achieved in 1947 – and with it the partition of the country and the separation of the railway system into Indian and Pakistani administrations – the introduction of new standard classes of locomotives was begun. The Pacific type had been selected by the Locomotive Standard Committee in the 1920s as permitting large fireboxes and grates suitable for low grades of coal, and light, intermediate and heavy designs of classes XA, XB and XC were produced for the broad-gauge lines. Corresponding YB Pacifics and ZB2-6-2s were evolved for the metre and narrow-gauge lines, while for freight work XD and even bigger XE2-8-2s for the broad gauge and smaller YD and ZE2-8-2s for the other gauges completed the range.

The Second World War saw the arrival of numbers of American locomotives supplied under Lend-Lease, and the first examples of the new standard design of Pacifics, the WP class, were ordered from Baldwin in the United States. Ultimately, a total of 755 WPs were built in a number of foreign countries as well as in India. The freight counterpart of the WP was the WG2-8-2, and as with the earlier classes there were metre gauge YP and YG equivalents. Again, indigenous production was supplemented by large orders from other countries, and the total of WGs alone reached 2,450.

For all the achievements of the builders of the 64,000km (40,000mls) Indian railway network, and of the administrators in running a transport system for so many people, the most famous of all India's railways is a little 61cm (2ft) gauge line that twists its way from Siliguri up into the foothills of the Himalayas and the old hill station of Darjeeling.

One distinctive feature of Chinese locomotives, inherited from the Soviet designs, is the prominent casing on top of the boiler which encloses a steam pipe leading forward from the dome to a regulator box which is sited on the smoke box behind the chimney. This casing is also apparent on the JS 2-8-2 Liberation and RM4-6-2 People classes. Like Indian locomotives, the Chinese engines display an attractive variety of ornamentation and decoration.

In the south Pacific, steam railways in Australia and New Zealand are now in the hands of the many preservation organizations, diesel and electric traction having taken over main-line operations.

The Australian railways were slow to develop in the early stages. A sparse population, concentrated in widely dispersed centres, and separate colonial administrations in six different regions, led to initial building of more or less local lines. More serious was an early agreement between Victoria, South Australia and New South Wales, which changed to standard gauge: the other two states, having already ordered broad gauge locomotives, went ahead with the agreed measure, so that when the first railways were opened in the 1850s there were two different gauges in use.

The situation became more complicated during the 1860s and 1870s, when the other states began building their first railways. Tasmania followed Victoria and South Australia in using the 160cm (5ft 3in) gauge, but Queensland and Western Australia went for economy of construction with yet a third gauge, this time of 106.7cm (3ft 6in), which was later applied to the Tasmanian system and to some lines built in South Australia.

The consequence of all this variety in gauges was that Victoria and South Australia were the only two colonies with a common border and the same gauge of railway. Moreover, full advantage was taken of the narrow gauge's opportunity for light track, relatively sharp grades and tight curves, so that subsequent development was restricted by the track within colonies as well as by the gauge changes between them.

The immense variety of locomotives that appeared, as imported models were supplemented by the various colonies' own production, is well represented by the numerous museums and preservation societies, and the same is true of New Zealand, where agreement over gauges hindered early building of railways.

Ultimately, New Zealand standardized on a gauge of 106.7cm (3ft 6in), and all lines were of this gauge by the end of the 1870s. The locomotives of this period were predominantly tank types, but in 1874 the first J class Canterbury Goods 2-6-0 tender engines were built. A total of 32 of these were acquired, and the last was not withdrawn from service until 1955.

The J class, like all locomotives used up to this period, were imported from England until the first indigenous types appeared. In the early years of the twentieth century, typical products included the B, Ba and Bb 4-8-0 goods engines, of which a total of 50 were built, the majority being the Bb type for passenger and mixed as well as goods services.

In 1906 one of the most successful of all New Zealand steam locomotive designs appeared in the shape of the A class Pacific, a four-cylinder compound on the de Glehn system. A total of 57 were built, and after a long career on the express services, some were still at work on coal trains when steam was finally superseded by diesel power on the west coast coal lines in 1969.

The Ab class, built in 1915, used superheating to dispense with the A class compound operation, and featured the novel Vanderbilt type of tender, which incorporated a cylindrical water tank. A total of 141 were built, mostly in New Zealand, with further examples supplied by the North British Locomotive company.

Later New Zealand types included the K class 4-8-4, designed to be the most powerful locomotive possible, given the rather restricted loading gauge on the New Zealand lines. The 30 original Ks were supplemented by the improved Ka and Kb classes; the latter added a booster unit for use on the most heavily graded sections on the South Island.

For the lighter rails used on secondary lines, the J class 4-8-2s appeared in 1939. In their original form, the J class were given an impressive style of streamlined casing, though this was later removed, and the later Ja class omitted it altogether. These were the last steam locomotives designed for New Zealand Railways, as the conversion to diesel operation began in

1948 with the first orders for diesel shunting engines, and the first main-line diesels followed two years later.

Early in the twentieth century, an Australian engineer, Herbert Garrat, developed a new system of articulation, which involved mounting the water tank and fuel bunker on separate engine units fore and aft of the boiler, which was carried between the two. As well as allowing the locomotive to pivot at two points, the Garrat system has a number of other advantages: a high adhesion weight is spread over a long wheelbase; a large diameter of boiler can be used; and the firebox grate can be deep and wide, since there are no wheels and axles underneath to limit its size. The Garrat system was developed by the British firm of Beyer-Peacock, and the Beyer-Garrat locomotive proved ideal for African conditions as soon as it was introduced in South Africa shortly after the First World War.

By the early part of the twentieth century, there were a number of alternative routes across North America. By acquiring the Chicago, Burlington and Quincy Railroad, James J. Hill, owner of the Northern Pacific and Great Northern lines, was able to complete the route from Chicago to Seattle and Portland over which the appropriately named Empire Builder service was inaugurated in 1929.

During the 1930s, many newly named trains were introduced in an effort to stem the loss of passengers that resulted from the growing use of private cars and the economic depression that followed the stock market collapse of 1929. By that time the Chicago and North Western and the Union Pacific had eradicated the bottleneck at Omaha by cooperating to run the City of San Francisco and City of Los Angeles services to California, while the City of Portland and City of Denver services served their respective cities, the latter service connecting with the Denver and Rio Grande Western's California Zephyr.

None of these services did anything to eradicate the need for a change at Chicago, and during the 1930s competition between the New York Central and Pennsylvania railroads was as fierce as ever. The respective prestige services on the two lines at that time were the Twentieth Century Limited and the Broadway Limited. In 1910 the Pennsylvania had opened its new station in the centre of New York, so that intending passengers no longer had to take a ferry from Manhattan Island to Jersey City before beginning their journey, and by the 1930s both railroads were running their fastest trains to Chicago in only 16 hours.

In the period between the two world wars, the North American passenger train developed to its finest form. The passenger cars were luxurious and the services provided were lavish. The names of the trains alone were associated with an aura of romance and adventure – Empire Builder, Chief, Daylight, Twentieth Century Limited – these and countless more became household words.

The Twentieth Century Limited, arguably the most famous of them all, served the 961 miles from New York to Chicago, and was introduced in 1902 by two railroads, the New York Central & Hudson River Railroad and the Lake Shore & Michigan Southern Railroad, which later became amalgamated as the New York Central system. The train was at first formed entirely of Pullman cars, convertible to sleepers at night.

The opening up of the western United States by the transcontinental railroads in the 1870s was mirrored in the following decade by the building of the Canadian Pacific. The construction of a transcontinental railway in Canada was actually embodied in the agreement by which the former independent colony of British Columbia became part of the Canadian federation in 1871. The original stipulation was that the line should be completed within 10 years, though it was another 15 years before the first trains were running between Montreal and the Pacific coast.

This was a formidable achievement, however, in view of the succession of mountain ranges in the west and the combination of rock and swamp with which the builders had to contend in their progress round the north of Lake Superior. The Canadian Pacific Railway grew to become one of the most successful rail operations in North America.

The other principle component of the Canadian railway system is Canadian National, which was formed after the First World War from a combination of government-owned lines and bankrupt private-enterprise systems. The competition between the two main systems has helped promote some excellent services on Canadian railways, and some outstanding locomotive designs.

Early locomotives were generally of the American 4-4-2 type, and, for the services between Montreal and Ottawa, Canadian Pacific produced a design of the Atlantic type 4-4-2 in 1899. These were four-cylinder compound engines, and they were able to operate 77.3km/h (48mph) services, including intermediate stops, between the two cities.

The dominant problem in Canadian railway operations, however, has always been the western mountain ranges. To deal with the climb through the

Kicking Horse Pass route, Canadian Pacific in 1929 produced the first of its famous class of 2-10-4 Selkirks.

Contemporary with the Selkirks were the most famous of all Canadian locomotives, the Hudsons. These were 4-6-4 passenger engines produced by the Montreal Locomotive Works, the same firm that built the Selkirks, and they were at their most impressive on the Montreal-Ottawa services, where they worked some of the fastest schedules in the world in the 1930s.

The very last CP steam locomotive to be built (1949), CP Selkirk No 5935 is shown taking on water at Fields BC in June 1952

GLOSSARY

Overall length: The length either over the buffers of the engine and tender or over the coupling faces where centre buffers are used

Total Weight: The total weight of engine and tender fully loaded

Cylinders: The number of cylinders is given first, followed by their diameter and stroke. Compound locomotives have both **HP** (high-pressure) and **LP** (low-pressure) cylinders, and details for each are given

Driving Wheels: Sizes given are for the diameter of the wheels as newly fitted

Axle Load: Figures quoted refer to the highest static load as applied to any pair of wheels on the rails. The axle load will vary according to the amount of coal and water in the boiler

Fuel: Unless otherwise stated, the fuel used is coal

Grate Area: The grate is usually formed of cast-iron bars on which the fire burns. The size of grate and thus the size of fire are important as they represent the source of the steam locomotive's power

Water: The amount given is the total amount carried in the tender and/or tanks

Heating Surface: The measure of the size of the boiler comprising the surface area of the fire tubes, the firebox and water tubes in the firebox

Superheater: The area given is that of the superheater elements

Steam Pressure: Intended working steam pressure of the boiler and the pressure at which the valves would be set to open

Adhesive Weight: The weight on the driving wheels of a locomotive on the rails, on which depend the grip between wheels and rail and the pulling power the locomotive can exert

Tractive Effort: This figure represents how hard the locomotive can pull when 85% of maximum boiler pressure is applied to the pistons

List of abbreviations

cm	centimetres
cw	hundredweight
ft	feet
in	inches
gal	gallons
kg	kilograms
kg/cm^2	kilograms per square centimetre
km	kilometre
km/h	kilometres per hour
lb	pounds
lit	litres
m	metres
m^2	square metres
ml	mile
mm	millimetres
mph	miles per hour
psi	pounds per square inch

STOURBRIDGE LION 0-4-0

Country of Origin: USA
Railway: Delaware & Hudson Canal Company (D&H)
Date: 1829
Length Overall: 3.924m (12ft 10.5in)
Cylinders: 2 215 × 914mm (8.5 × 36in)

Driving Wheels: 1.244m (4ft 1in)
Axle Load: 3,920kg (8,624lbs)
Adhesive Weight: 7,127kg (15,680lb) excluding tender
History: Making its first run on 9 August 1829 at Honesdale, Pennsylvania, the *Stourbridge Lion*, which had been built by the British Company of Foster & Rastrick, ran on a 1.295m (4ft 3in) gauge tramway operated by the Delaware & Hudson Canal Company. The *Stourbridge Lion* made its one and only run without a train and with only master mechanic Horatio Allen on the platform. Following this outing, the *Lion* was considered to be grossly overweight and unsuitable for service as a locomotive, and it spent the remainder of its working life as a stationary engine. A replica of the locomotive is at the Smithsonian Museum, Washington DC.

NORTHUMBRIAN 0-2-2

Country of Origin: Great Britain
Railway: Liverpool & Manchester Railway (L&M)
Date: 1830
Length Overall: 7.315m (24ft)
Total Weight: 11,590kg (25,500lb)
Cylinders: 2 280 × 406mm (11 × 16in)
Driving Wheels: 1.321m (4ft 4in)
Axle Load: 2,955kg (6,500lb)
Fuel: 1,000kg (2,200lb) coke
Grate Area: 0.75m² (8sq ft)
Water: 1,817lit (400gal) (480 US gal)
Heating Surface: 38m² (412sq ft)
Steam Pressure: 3.5kg/cm² (50psi)
Adhesive Weight: 2,955kg (6,500lb)
Tractive Effort: 720kg (1,580lb)

History: The world's first inter-city steam railway opened on 15 September 1830, and the first train was hauled by the *Northumbrian*. It is from the fundamental basis of this steam engine that virtually all steam locomotives since built derived.

PLANET CLASS 2-2-0

Country of Origin: Great Britain
Railway: Liverpool & Manchester Railway
Date: 1830
Length Overall: 7.42m (24ft 4in)
Total Weight: 13,409kg (29,500lb)
Cylinders: 2 292 × 406mm (11.5 × 16in)
Driving Wheels: 1.575m (5ft 2in)
Axle Load: 5,113kg (11,250lb)
Fuel: 1,000kg (2,200lb) coke
Grate Area: 0.67m² (7.2sq ft)
Water: 1,817lit (400gal) (480 US gal)
Heating Surface: 38m² (407sq ft)
Steam Pressure: 3.5kg/cm² (50psi)
Adhesive Weight: 5,113kg (11,250lb)
Tractive Effort: 660kg (1,450lb)

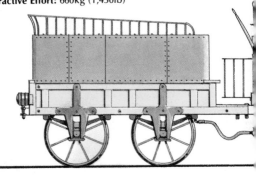

History: Stephenson's Planet Class followed immediately after the *Northumbrian* on the Liverpool and Manchester Railway in 1830.

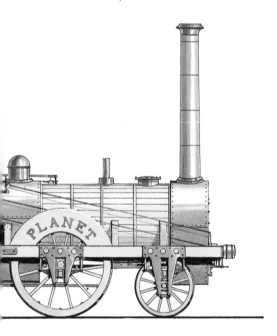

JOHN BULL 4-2-0

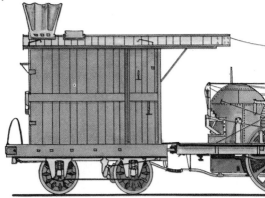

Country of Origin: USA
Railway: Camden & Amboy Railroad
Date: 1831
Length Overall: 11.277m (37ft)
Cylinders: 2 228 × 508mm (9 × 20in)
Driving Wheels: 1.371m (4ft 6in)
Grate Area: 0.9m² (10sq ft)
Heating Surface: 28m² (300sq ft)
Steam Pressure: 2.1kg/cm² (30psi)
Adhesive Weight: 20,036kg (44,080lb)
Tractive Effort: 347kg (765lb)

History: British-built by the Stephensons at New-castle-upon-Tyne, the *John Bull* made its first exhibition run on 12 November 1831. It was re-assembled in New Jersey by the Camden & Amboy's master mechanic, Isaac Dripps, who added for the first time to any locomotive the headlight, bell and cow catcher. The locomotive started regular steam operation the following year and remained in service until 1866. In 1893 it was exhibited at the Chicago Exposition, travelling there under its own steam. The *John Bull* is now exhibited at the Smithsonian Museum, Washington DC.

VAUXHALL 2-2-0

Country of Origin: Ireland
Railway: Dublin & Kingstown Railway
Date: 1834
(Approximate Specification)
Length Overall: 7.315m (24ft)
Cylinders: 2 280 × 457mm (11 × 18in)
Driving Wheels: 1.524m (5ft)
Steam Pressure: 3.5kg/cm² (50psi)
Tractive Effort: 700kg (1,550lb)
History: Built by George Forrester of Liverpool, the *Vauxhall* was the first locomotive to have accessible outside cylinders placed horizontally, a feature that has been standard ever since. A second innovation of Forrester was the valve gear. The 'slip-electric' previously used was difficult to reverse from the cab; Forrester developed a separate eccentric set for each cylinder for each direction – a total of four in each

axle. The covering lever moved the eccentric rods, engaging the valve pin by means of V-shaped groups. The *Vauxhall* was built to the standard English gauge of 1,435mm (4ft 8in) and is reported to have achieved a speed of 50km/h (31mph) on its inaugural trip in Ireland. In order to achieve a smoother ride the 2-2-0s were converted to 2-2-2s for the London & Greenwich Railway.

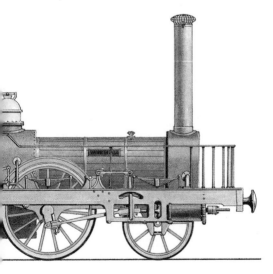

ADLER 2-2-2

Country of Origin: Germany
Railway: Nuremberg-Fürth Railway
Date: 1835
Length Overall: 7.62m (25ft)
Total Weight: 14,318kg (31,500lb) (engine only)
Cylinders: 229 × 406mm (9 × 16in)
Driving Wheels: 1.371m (4ft 6in)
Axle Load: 6,022kg (13,250lb)
Grate Area: 0.48m² (5.2sq ft)
Heating Surface: 18.2m² (196sq ft)
Steam Pressure: 4.2kg/cm² (60psi)
Adhesive Weight: 6,022kg (13,250lb)
Tractive Effort: 550kg (1,220lb)
History: Ludwig I of Bavaria gave his royal assent for a railway to be built in 1834. Known as the Ludwigsbahn, it was to run from Nuremberg to Fürth. On

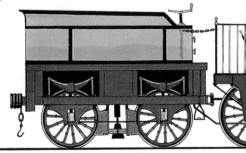

7 December 1835 the line was opened, inaugurated by a locomotive built by Robert Stephenson & Co. for the sum of £1,750 and known as *Der Adler* or *Adler* (Eagle). The engine, a 2-2-2, resembles the Stephensons' *Patentee* of 1833 in that the driving wheels had no flanges, thereby relieving a great deal of pressure from the crank.

BURY 2-2-0

Country of Origin: Great Britain
Railway: London & Birmingham Railway (L&B)
Date: 1837
Length Overall: 8.168m (26ft 9.5in)
Total Weight: 10,000kg (22,000lb)
Cylinders: 2 280 × 415mm (11 × 16.5in)
Driving Wheels: 1.546m (5ft 0.75in)
Axle Load: 5,727kg (12,600lb)
Fuel: 1,000kg (2,200lb) coke
Grate Area: 0.65m² (7sq ft)
Water: 1.817lit (400gal) (480 US gal)
Heating Surface: 33.2m² (357sq ft)
Steam Pressure: 3.5kg/cm² (50psi)
Adhesive Weight: 5,727kg (12,600lb)
Tractive Effort: 629kg (1,386lb)
History: Cheap to build and reliable in service, Bury supplied 58 of these underpowered 2-2-0 locomotives to the London-Birmingham Railway by 1841. The

engine should have been completed in time for the Rainhill trials, but Bury was too late, subsequently selling his first engine, named *Liverpool*, to the Liverpool & Manchester Railway in 1830. The bar-framed Bury had large coupled wheels 1,829mm (72in) in diameter, but was limited by the size of its D-shaped fire box, making it impossible to enlarge the locomotive. Bury supplied some of his bar-framed locomotives to North America, and this type of construction became more widely used there until replaced by cast steel.

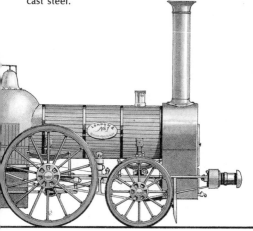

LAFAYETTE 4-2-0

Country of Origin: USA
Railway: Baltimore & Ohio Railroad (B&O)
Date: 1837
Length Overall: 9.25m (30ft 4in)
Total Weight: 20,000kg (44,000lb)
Cylinders: 2 268 × 457mm (10.5 × 18in)
Driving Wheels: 1.22m (4ft)
Axle Load: 5,909kg (13,000lb)
Fuel: 1,000kg (2,200lb)
Grate Area: 0.8m² (8.6sq ft)
Water: 2,045lit (450gal) (540 US gal)
Heating Surface: 36.6m² (394sq ft)
Steam Pressure: 4.2 kg/cm² (60psi)
Adhesive Weight: 13,636kg (30,000lb)
Tractive Effort: 957kg (2,162lb)
History: The William Norris-built Lafayette 4-2-0 was a great success, providing a good performance at a low

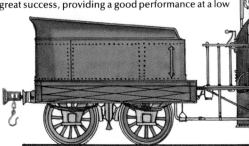

52

fuel cost. The locomotives, which were reliable and needed few repairs, incorporated for the first time a combination of developments initially seen in other locomotives: Northumbrian outside cylinders; Planet cylinders at the front; bar trims from the Bury; and the bogie from Brother Jonathan – a huge step forward towards the final form of the steam passenger locomotive. The Norris locomotives were extremely popular and widely exported, first to Canada (Champlain & St. Lawrence Railway), then to Vienna (Raab Railway) in 1837, and later to Germany and Britain.

LION 0-4-2

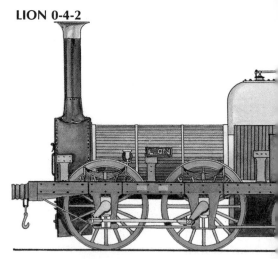

Country of Origin: Great Britain
Railway: Liverpool & Manchester Railway (L&M)
Date: 1838
Length Overall: 10.287m (33ft 9in)
Cylinders: 2 305 × 457mm (12 × 18in)
Driving Wheels: 1.524m (5ft)
Steam Pressure: 3.5kg/cm² (50psi)
Tractive Effort: 833kg (1,836lb)
History: Built by Todd, Kitson & Laird of Leeds, the

Lion is the world's oldest working locomotive. The Liverpool & Manchester Railway sold the *Lion* to Mersey Docks and Harbour Board in 1859, where she was

used as a shunting engine. The Board later established her as a stationary engine, in which form she remained operative until 1920. LMS Railway bought the *Lion* and restored her, running her in the 1930 centenary celebration of the Liverpool & Manchester Railway before handing her over to the Merseyside County Museum at Liverpool. The *Lion* was turned out again in 1980, to run in the cavalcade to celebrate the 150th anniversary of the L&M.

FIRE FLY CLASS 2-2-2

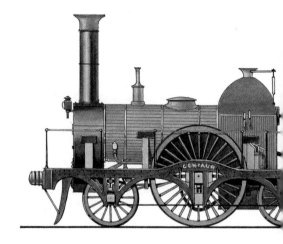

Country of Origin: Great Britain
Railway: Great Western Railway (GWR)
Date: 1840
Length Overall: 12m (39ft 4in)
Total Weight: 42,045kg (92,500lb)
Cylinders: 2 381 × 457mm (15 × 18in)
Driving wheels: 2.134m (7ft)
Axle Load: 11,363kg (25,000lb)

Fuel: 1,545kg (3,400lb) coke
Grate Area: 1.25m² (13.5sq ft)
Water: 8,280lit (1,800gal) (2,160 US gal)
Heating Surface: 65m² (700sq ft)
Steam Pressure: 3.5kg/cm² (50psi)
Adhesive Weight: 11,363kg (25,000lb)
Tractive Effort: 929kg (2,049lb)
History: Brainchild of Daniel Gooch, a one-time employee of the Stephensons, the Fire Fly Class was for 40 years the saviour of Brunel's 2.14m (7ft 0.25in)

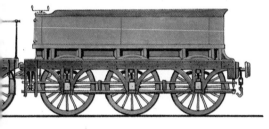

broad gauge. Sixty-two locomotives were built by six companies by 1842 and the first of these, *Fire Fly*, built by Jones, Turner and Evans, reached a maximum speed of 93km/h (58mph) on 17 March 1840. Another engine, *Phlegethon*, pulled the first Royal Train for Queen Victoria from Slough to Paddington on 13 June 1842. The last engine was withdrawn from service in 1879.

BEUTH 2-2-2

Country of Origin: Germany
Railway: Berlin-Anhalt Railway
Date: 1843
Length Overall: 6.143m (20ft 2in) engine only
Total Weight: 9,091kg (20,000lb)
Cylinders: 2 330 × 560mm (13 × 22in)
Driving Wheels: 1.543m (5ft 0.75in)
Axle Load: 9.091kg (20,000lb)
Grate Area: 0.83m² (8.9sq ft)
Heating Surface: 47m² (500sq ft)

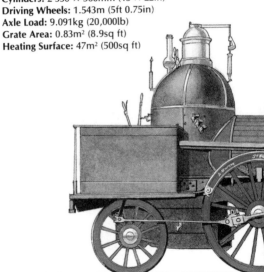

Steam Pressure: 5.5kg/cm² (78psi)
Adhesive Weight: 9,091kg (20,000lb)
Tractive effort: 1,870kg (4,120lb)
History: Designed and built by August Börsig of Berlin, the Beuth incorporated all the latest developments from Germany, Great Britain and the USA.

MUD-DIGGER 0-8-0

Country of Origin: USA
Railway: Baltimore & Ohio Railroad (B&O)
Date: 1844
Length Overall: 6.045m (19ft 10in) excluding tender
Total Weight: 21,363kg (47,000lb) excluding tender
Cylinders: 2 432 × 610mm (1.7 × 24in)
Driving Wheels: 0.838m (2ft 9in)
Axle Load: 5,875kg (12,925lb)
Adhesive Weight: 21,363kg (47,000lb)

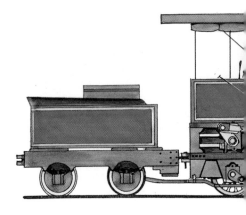

History: Given the name 'Mud-Digger' because they used to stir up the stones and dirt due to their low cranks, the locomotives were the invention of one Ross Winans, who patented his first design, known as 'Winan's Crab', in 1837. His first 0-8-0, named *Hercules*, was delivered to B&O in 1844, and by 1847 another 13 had been delivered with the last, No.41 *Elk*, remaining in service until 1880. The Mud-Diggers had horizontal cylinders and a proper locomotive boiler, whereas their two 1838-built 0-4-0 Crab predecessors had vertical boilers.

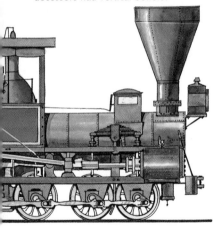

JOHN STEVENS 6-2-0

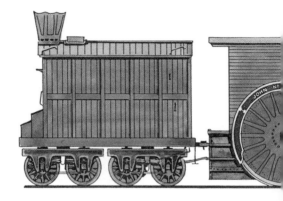

Country of Origin: USA
Railway: Camden & Amboy Railroad
Date: 1849
Length Overall: 9.042m (29ft 8in) excluding tender
Total Weight: 22,727kg (50,000lb) excluding tender
Cylinders: 2. 330 × 863mm (13 × 34in)
Driving Wheels: 2.438mm (8ft)
Grate Area: 11.4m² (15.2 sq ft)
History: This strange-looking locomotive was the first of seven built by Norris & Co. Based primarily on the Thomas Russell Crampton engines employed in

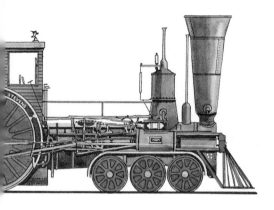

France and Belgium in the 1840s, the John Stevens had one pair of very large driving wheels which enabled the locomotive to move very fast, but it lacked adhesive weight. The driving wheels were of wrought iron with wood infills between the spokes. Further specification details are not available, but the small grate area and firebox would have led to lack of steam pressure. All seven locomotives were converted to 4-4-0s before their withdrawal in 1860. The John Stevens ran on a 1.435m (4ft 8.5in) standard gauge.

CRAMPTON TYPE 4-2-0

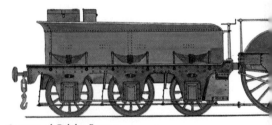

Country of Origin: France
Railway: Eastern Railways (Est)
Date: 1852
Length Overall: 12.728m (41ft 9in)
Total Weight: 47,727kg (105,000lb)
Cylinders: 2 400 × 500mm (15.75 × 21.5in)
Driving Wheels: 2.1m (6ft 10.75in)
Axle Load: 12,500kg (27,500lb)
Fuel: 7,045kg (15,500lb)
Grate Area: 1.42m² (15.3sq ft)
Water: 7,084lit (1,540gal) (1,850 US gal)
Heating Surface: 98.4m² (1,059sq ft)
Steam Pressure: 6.5kg/cm² (92psi)
Adhesive Weight: 12,318kg (27,100lb)
Tractive Effort: 2,290kg (5,040lb)

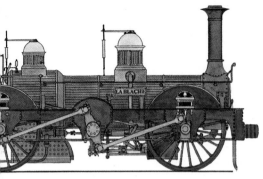

History: Over 300 Cramptons were built, the first of which, the *Namur*, was for the Belgian Namur-Liége Railway. Thomas Russell Crampton was born in 1816, and in 1842 was working with Daniel Gooch for the GWR when he patented his high-speed express locomotive. On 20 June 1890 a rebuilt Crampton of Eastern Railways broke the world speed record at 114km/h (89.5mph). Easy access to the well-balanced mechanism and long periods of trouble-free running contributed to the popularity of these 4-2-0s, which were designed for fast running of light loads. Crampton also patented his highly successful throttle valve. No. 80 *Le Continent* is still in working condition, and is on exhibition at the French National Railway Museum at Mulhouse.

PEARSON 9FT SINGLE CLASS 4-2-4

Country of Origin: Great Britain
Railway: Bristol & Exeter Railway (B&ER)
Date: 1854
Length Overall: 9.372m (30ft 9in)
Total Weight: 50,909kg (112,000lb)
Cylinders: 2 457 × 610mm (18 × 24in)
Driving Wheels: 2.743m (8ft 10in)
Axle Load: 18,863kg (41,500lb)
Fuel: 2,036kg (4,480lb)
Grate Area: 2.15m² (23sq ft)
Water: 6,592lit (1,430gal) (1,720 US gal)
Heating Surface: 114.8m² (1,235sq ft)
Steam Pressure: 8.4kg/cm² (120psi)
Adhesive Weight: 18,863kg (41,500lb)

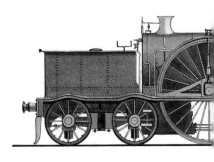

Tractive Effort: 3,330kg (7,344lb)

History: Eight Pearson 4-2-4 tank locomotives were built by Rothwell & Co. of Bolton in 1853/54, four of them being rebuilt in 1868. Cylinders and motion were inside the frame, and the engine was guided by a four-wheeled bogie on either side of a pair of enormous driving wheels, the largest ever on a working locomotive. Water was carried in a well tank between the frames in addition to a tank at the rear. Built for the broad gauge, and specifically to haul what was then the fastest train in the world, the Flying Dutchman, along the Bristol & Exeter Railways section, a speed of 130km/h (81.8mph) was recorded, at the time a world steam locomotive record.

AMERICAN TYPE 4-4-0

Country of Origin: USA
Railway: Western & Atlantic Railroad (W&ARR)
Date: 1855
Length Overall: 15.926m (52ft 3in)
Total Weight: 40,909kg (90,000lb)

Cylinders: 2 381 × 610mm (15 × 24in)
Driving Wheels: 1.524m (5ft)
Axle Load: 9,545kg (21,000lb)
Fuel: 7.25m³ (256cu ft) wood
Grate Area: 1.35m² (14.5sq ft)
Water: 5,762lit (1,250gal) (2,000 US gal)
Heating Surface: 91m² (98sq ft)
Steam Pressure: 6.35kg/cm² (90psi)
Adhesive Weight: 19,545kg (43,000lb)
Tractive Effort: 3,123kg (6,885lb)
History: More American Type 4-4-0s were built than any other locomotive. The first was built by Thomas Rogers in 1855, although many builders were later to

follow the design, which made full use of Stephenson's link motion. The 25,000 or so American Standard locomotives completely dominated railroading in North America until the turn of the century, with some engines still in use in the 1950s, over a century after their first introduction. They were employed by all of the American railroads of the day for all duties under all conditions. They featured in the form of Union Pacific's No. 119 and Central Pacific's *Jupiter* at Promontory Point, Utah, at the famous last spike ceremony marking the completion of the first transcontinental railroad.

MEDOC CLASS 2-4-0

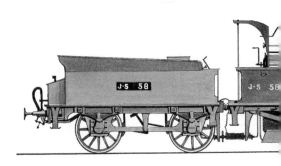

Country of Origin: Switzerland
Railway: Swiss Western Railway (O-S)
Date: 1857
Length Overall: 13.65m (44ft 9.5in)
Total Weight: 40,227kg (88,500lb)
Cylinders: 2 408 × 612mm (16 × 24in)
Driving Wheels: 1.686m (5ft 6.25in)
Axle Load: 9,159kg (20,150lb)
Fuel: 2,400kg (5,280lb)
Grate Area: 1.0m² (10.75sq ft)
Water: 4,056lit (880gal) (1,050 US gal)

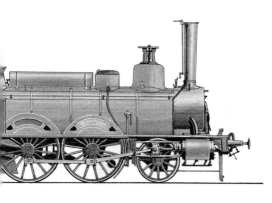

Heating Surface: 95m² (1,023sq ft)
Steam Pressure: 8kg/cm² (114psi)
Adhesive Weight: 18,181kg (40,000lb)
Tractive Effort: 4,077kg (8,986lb)
History: Built between 1856 and 1858 at Karlsruhe, Germany, 15 were supplied to the Swiss Western Railway, the last being withdrawn from service in 1902 from what had become the Jura-Simplon Railway (J-S). The *Medoc* was a standard engine of the day, being a long-boiler six-wheeled design of Robert Stephenson & Co. made under licence.

CONSOLIDATION 2-8-0
Country of Origin: USA

Railway: Lehigh Valley & Mahoney Railroad (L&MRR)
Date: 1866
Length Overall: 10.312m (33ft 10in) excluding tender
Total Weight: 45,454kg (100,000lb) excluding tender
Cylinders: 2 508 × 609mm (20 × 24in)
Driving Wheels: 1.219m (4ft)
Axle Load: 11,000kg (24,200lb)
Grate Area: 2.6m² (27.6sq ft)
Heating Surface: 119m² (1,281sq ft)
Steam Pressure: 9.1kg/cm² (130psi)
Adhesive Weight: 40,000kg (88,000lb)
Tractive Effort: 9,556kg (21,061lb)

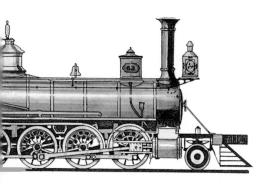

History: Designed for heavy freight work, and especially for steep gradients and tight curves, the first Consolidation was delivered in 1866 to Lehigh Valley Railroad at the time of its formation by the amalgamation of several small railroads in the area. These very sturdy, Baldwin-built locomotives had each cylinder casting integral with half the smokebox saddle, and the two centre pairs of driving wheels were flangeless. The connecting rods drove on the third axle. 1866 was also the year in which America's greatest locomotive manufacturer, Mathias Baldwin, died at the age of 70.

STIRLING 8FT SINGLE CLASS 4-2-2

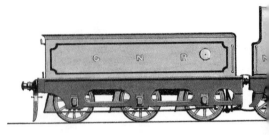

Country of Origin: Great Britain
Railway: Great Northern Railway (GNR)
Date: 1870
Length Overall: 15.24m (50ft 2in)
Total Weight: 66,136kg (145,500lb)
Cylinders: 2 457 × 711mm (18 × 28in)
Driving Wheels: 2.463m (8ft 1in)
Axle Load: 15,454kg (34,000lb)
Fuel: 3,409kg (7,500lb)
Grate Area: 1.64m² (17.65sq ft)
Water: 13,369lit (2,900gal) (3,480 US gal)
Heating Surface: 108m² (1,165sq ft)
Steam Pressure: 9.8kg/cm² (140psi)
Adhesive Weight: 15,727kg (34,600lb)
Tractive Effort: 5,101kg (11,245lb)

History: The most beautiful of steam locomotives, the Stirling 8ft Single was built at GNR's Doncaster workshop to the order of GNR's Locomotive Superintendent, Patrick Stirling. Forty-seven were built in total over a period of 23 years, with the last being withdrawn from service in 1916. No. 1, the first built, now resides at the National Railway Museum, York. The locomotive has outside cylinders with inside valve chests. Slide valves are driven by sets of Stephenson's link motion. Employed on the prestigious Flying Scotsman route from London Kings Cross to Edinburgh, the Stirling No. 1 was the first ever museum piece to be chartered for enthusiasts' pleasure runs when it was so used in 1938 on a **run from** Kings Cross to Cambridge.

DUKE CLASS 4-4-0

Country of Origin: Great Britain
Railway: Highland Railway (HR)
Date: 1874
Length Overall: 15.62m (51ft 3in)
Total Weight: 73,409kg (161,500lb)
Cylinders: 2 457 × 610mm (18 × 24in)
Driving Wheels: 1.92m (6ft 3.5in)
Axle Load: 14,318kg (31,500lb)
Fuel: 4091kg (9,000lb)
Grate Area: 1.51m² (16.25sq ft)
Water: 8,298lit (1,800gal) (2,160 US gal)
Heating Surface: 114m² (1,228sq ft)
Steam Pressure: 9.84kg/cm² (140psi)
Adhesive Weight: 27,045kg (59,500lb)
Tractive Effort: 5,597kg (12,338lb)

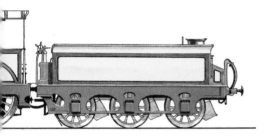

History: Only ten of these beautiful 4-4-0s were built, the last of which, *Duke*, gave its name to the class, although it was later renamed *Cromartie*. Built in Glasgow by Dubs, they entered service in 1874, the last being withdrawn almost half a century later in 1923. The engines featured Alexander Allan's straight-link valve gear, and introduced for the first time the louvered chimney, designed to throw the smoke clear over the cab, in addition to assisting with the draughting. The double frame arrangement of the Duke had appeared before on previous HR engines and added to the strength of the structure necessary for the rigours of pulling the train across the mountains of Scotland.

CLASS 121 2-4-2
Country of Origin: France

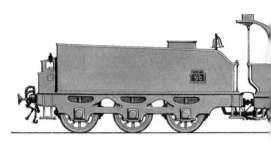

Railway: Paris, Lyons & Mediterranean Railway (PLM)
Date: 1876
Length Overall: 17.2m (56ft 5in)
Total Weight: 49,790kg (109,539lb)
Cylinders: 2 500 × 650mm (19.7 × 23.7in)
Driving Wheels: 2.1m (6ft 10.5in)
Axle Load: 14,091kg (31,000lb)
Grate Area: 2.2m² (23sq ft)
Heating Surface: 119m² (1,280sq ft)
Steam Pressure: 9kg/cm² (129psi)
Adhesive Weight: 27,727kg (61,000lb)
Tractive Effort: 5,545kg (12,225lb)
History: The Paris, Lyons & Mediterranean Railway
had depended upon Crampton-type 4-2-0 engines
until 1868, when, driven by the need for greater

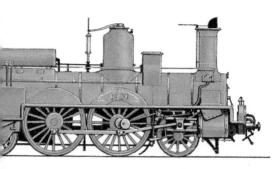

power, they built 50 2-4-0s with long boilers. However, these locomotives did not fulfill the need and the 2-4-0s were enlarged and rebuilt with an extra axle to become 2-4-2s. The extra stability achieved persuaded PLM to build 60 new 2-4-2s. Designated Class 121, they incorporated a Belpaire firebox and Gooch's valve gear. A further 300 were built, including 40 built in Manchester by Sharp, Steward & Co., and these very successful locomotives worked a greatly mixed variety of traffic, remaining in use until about 1950. The final batch of engines were compound locomotives built with Walschaert's valve gear, and boilers with a designed steam pressure of 15kg/cm^2 (214psi). A restored Class 121 is exhibited at the Mulhouse National Railway Museum.

C-16-60 2-8-0

Country of Origin: USA
Railway: Denver & Rio Grande Railroad (D&RG)
Date: 1882
Length Overall: 17.189m (56ft 4.75in)

Total Weight: 50,727kg (111,600lb)
Cylinders: 2 381 × 508mm (15 × 20in)
Driving Wheels: 0.939mm (3ft 1in)
Axle Load: 6,280kg (13,818lb)
Fuel: 5,454kg (12,000lb)
Grate Area: 1.3m² (14sq ft)
Water: 9,464lit (2,083gal) (2,500 US gal)
Heating Surface: 77m² (834sq ft)
Steam Pressure: 11.3kg/cm² (160psi)
Adhesive Weight: 22,841kg (50,250lb)
Tractive Effort: 7,623kg (16,800lb)

History: The Denver & Rio Grande Railroad, inaugurated in 1876 by General William Jackson Palmer, was built to the narrow gauge of 0.914m (3ft) and ran extensively throughout Colorado, basically serving the silver mining communities. To reach the altitudes of 2,865m (9,400ft) at La Veta Pass via a route of 1-in-25 inclines and 30° turns, the D&RG invested in 131 Baldwin-built 2-8-0 locomotives. The engines had slide valves above the cylinders and Stephenson's link motion, and sported polished brass work and Russian iron boiler cladding.

VITTORIO EMANUELE II 4-6-0

Country of Origin: Italy
Railway: Upper Italy Railroads (SFAI)

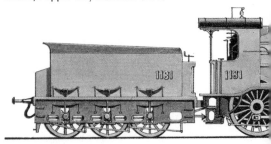

Date: 1884
Length Overall: 16.5m (54ft 1.5in)
Total Weight: 83,852kg (184,475lb)
Cylinders: 2 470 × 620mm (18.5 × 24.5in)
Driving Wheels: 1.675m (5ft 6in)
Axle Load: 16,136kg (35,500lb)
Fuel: 3,500kg (7,700lb)
Grate Area: 2,25m² (24sq ft)
Water: 10,142lit (2,200gal) (2,630 US gal)
Heating Surface: 124m² (1,720sq ft)
Steam Pressure: 10kg/cm² (142psi)
Adhesive Weight: 48,181kg (106,000lb)
Tractive Effort: 6,958kg (15,335lb)

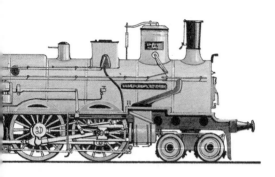

History: The 55 locomotives built between 1884 and 1896 included the very first European 4-6-0, Vittorio Emanuele II. Designed to pull 125-tonne trains up the Giovi Pass incline on the Turin-Genoa line, they were the last locomotives designed by the Upper Italy Railroads before they were absorbed into the Mediterranean System in 1885. The locomotives were built in Munich as well as in Milan and Genoa, and then made use of Gooch's valve gear outside the wheels in preference to Stephenson's gear. Unhappily, the Vittorio Emanuele class have a place in history as the first main-line steam locomotives to be replaced by electric track when the Giovi line was converted in 1910.

JOHNSON MIDLAND SINGLE 4-2-2

Country of Origin: Great Britain
Railway: Midland Railway (MR)
Date: 1887

Length Overall: 16.038m (52ft 7.5in)
Total Weight: 82,500kg (181,500lb)
Cylinders: 2 483 × 660mm (19 × 26in)
Driving Wheels: 2.375m (7ft 11.5in)
Axle Load: 17,954kg (39,500lb)
Fuel: 4,000kg (8,800lb)
Grate Area: 1.82m² (19.6sq ft)
Water: 15,902lit (3,500gal) (4,200 US gal)
Heating Surface: 115m² (1,237sq ft)
Steam Pressure: 12kg/cm² (170psi)
Adhesive Weight: 17,950kg (39,500lb)
Tractive Effort: 6,582kg (14,506lb)

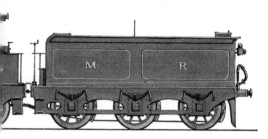

History: Ninety-five of these colourful single-wheelers were built, designed by S.W. Johnson, the first batch being built at the Midland Railway's Derby Works. Kept to a very high standard of cleanliness and mechanical order, these comparatively low-powered locomotives managed their duties admirably, pulling standard trains of 200-250 tonnes, with trains of 350 tonnes and speeds of 144km/h (90mph) being recorded. They had two sets of main motion plus two sets of Stephenson's valve gear and steam sanding gear, which reliably applied sand under the driving wheels.

TEUTONIC CLASS 2-2-2-0

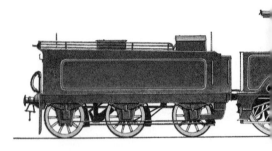

Country of Origin: Great Britain
Railway: London & North Western Railway (LNWR)
Date: 1889
Length Overall: 15.552m (51ft 0.25in)
Total Weight: 71,818kg (158,000lb)
Cylinders: HP:2 356 × 610mm (14 × 24in); LP:1 762 × 610mm (30 × 24in)
Driving Wheels: 2.159m (7ft 1in)
Axle Load: 15,909kg (35,000lb)
Fuel: 5,000kg (11,000lb)
Grate Area: 1.9m² (20.5sq ft)
Water: 8,172lit (1,800gal) (2,160 US gal)

Heating Surface: 130m² (1,402sq ft)
Steam Pressure: 12.3kg/cm² (175psi)
Adhesive Weight: 31,590kg (69,500lb)
History: Like the other Webb LNWR compounds, the ten Teutonic Class 2-2-2-0 compounds were never very successful. They were difficult to get going, needing men with pinch bars to give them an initial starting movement, and in addition to that they were not economical to run. The Teutonics were probably the best of Webb's compounds, employing a slip eccentric in place of Joy's valve gear of earlier 2-2-2-0s.

NO. 999 4-4-0

Country of Origin: USA
Railway: New York Central & Hudson River Railroad
(NYC&HRRR)

Date: 1893
Length Overall: 17.63m (57ft 10in)
Total Weight: 38,181kg (84,000lb)
Cylinders: 2 483 × 610mm (19 × 24in)
Driving Wheels: 2. 184m (7ft 2in)
Axle Load: 19,091kg (42,000lb)
Fuel: 7,000kg (15,400lb)
Grate Area: 2.85m² (30.7sq ft)
Water: 13,393lit (2,950gal) (3,500 US gal)
Heating Surface: 179m² (1,927sq ft)
Steam Pressure: 12.6kg/cm² (190psi)
Adhesive Weight: 38,181kg (84,000lb)
Tractive Effort: 7,382 kg (16,270lb)

History: The forerunner of the Twentieth Century Limited, the Empire State Express pulled by No. 999s was designed to run between New York and Chicago in a scheduled 20 hours for the 1,536km (960mls). Specially built at West Albany with Stephenson's valve gear and slide valves, No. 999 set a standard of luxury and speed unrivalled anywhere in the world. In 1893 an unconfirmed speed of 180km/h (112.5mph) between two mileposts was reported by the conductor, a speed that, if correct, would have been a world speed record for any form of transport.

CLASS Q1 4-4-0

Country of Origin: Great Britain
Railway: North Eastern Railway (NER)
Date: 1896
Length Overall: 17.145m (50ft 3in)
Total Weight: 93,636kg (206,000lb)
Cylinders: 2 508 × 660mm (20 × 26in)
Driving Wheels: 2.315m (7ft 7.25in)
Axle Load: 19,091kg (42,000lb)
Fuel: 5,091kg (11,200lb) coal
Grate Area: 1.93m² (20.75sq ft)
Water: 18,160lit (4,000gal) (4,800 US gal)
Heating Surface: 113m² (1,216sq ft)
Steam Pressure: 12.3kg/cm² (175psi)
Adhesive Weight: 35,000kg (77,000lb)
Tractive Effort: 7,690kg (16,953lb)
History: The Class Q1 locomotives were purpose-built for a job they were never employed to do. Since

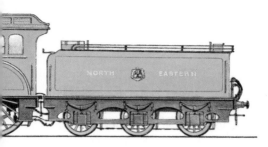

1888 the east and west-coast companies had raced each other daily from Kings Cross and Euston to Edinburgh, and the journey time of these races had dropped to between 8hrs 30min and 8hrs 40min. From 1895, the London-Aberdeen route was raced at night with the west-coast route supplying the slightly quicker service. NER planned to build five Class Q1 4-4-0 locomotives specially designed with very large coupled driving wheels, Stephenson's valve gear driving slide valves positioned on top of the cylinders, and Westinghouse air breaks. A large comfortable cab was also provided. Unfortunately, a derailment at high speed near Preston on the west-coast route called an end to the racing, and the Class Q1 locomotives were never raced. In the event, only two of the five were built, and these were withdrawn from top passenger work in 1903.

NO. 382 4-6-0

Country of Origin: USA
Railway: Illinois Central Railroad (ICRR)
Date: 1896
Length Overall: 18.364m (60ft 3in)
Total Weight: 93,431kg (205,550lb)
Cylinders: 2 495 × 660m (19.5 × 26in)
Driving Wheels: 1.752m (5ft 9in)
Axle Load: 16,783kg (36,923lb)
Fuel: 8,181kg (18,000lb)
Grate Area: 2.9m² (31.5sq ft)
Water: 18,928lit (4,166gal) (5,000 US gal)
Heating Surface: 176m² (1,892sq ft)

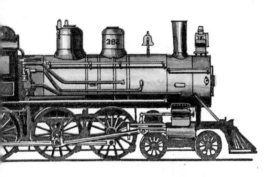

Steam Pressure: 12.7kg/cm² (180psi)
Adhesive Weight: 45,772kg (100,700lb)
Tractive Effort: 9,950kg (21,930lb)
History: Immortalized in the song 'The Cannonball Express', No. 382 and its driver Casey Jones one night in April 1900 at Vaughan, Mississippi, ran headlong into the rear of a slower train. Casey Jones was killed. No. 382 was rebuilt to continue for many years, serving on the Chicago-New Orleans route. Built at Paterson, New Jersey, by the Rogers Locomotive Works, No. 382 has Stephenson's valve gear and outside slide valves and a large impressive cab and roof.

LYN 2-4-2T

Country of Origin: USA
Railway: Lynton & Barnstaple Railway (L&B)

Date: 1898
Length Overall: 7.162m (23ft 6in)
Total Weight: 2,400kg (5,280lb)
Cylinders: 2 254 × 406mm (10 × 16in)
Driving Wheels: 0.838m (2ft 9in)
Axle Load: 7,127kg (15,680lb)
Grate Area: 0.7m² (7.7sq ft)
Water: 3,030lit (667gal) (800 US gal)
Heating Surface: 35m² (379sq ft)
Steam Pressure: 12.7kg/cm² (180psi)
Adhesive Weight: 14,254kg (31,360lb)
Tractive Effort: 3,364kg (7,415lb)

History: Built in the USA by Baldwin for the 30km (19mls) long British narrow-gauge Lynton & Barnstaple Railway (600mm/1ft 11.6in gauge), the *Lyn* was ordered, built and delivered in just three months. A one-off, in the normal Baldwin style the Lyn bore no number on the smoke box. L&B was merged into the Southern Railway in 1923 and *Lyn* was painted in the green livery, in which she is depicted above, and given a new US-style chimney in place of the original British copper-capped type. *Lyn* was scrapped in 1935 when the Lynton & Barnstaple line was closed.

CLASS 500 4-6-0

Country of Origin: Italy
Railway: Adriatic System (RA)
Date: 1900
Length Overall: 24.135m (79ft 2in)
Total Weight: 100,454kg (221,000lb)
Cylinders: HP: 2 370 × 650mm (14 × 25in); LP: 2 580 × 650mm (23 × 25in)
Driving Wheels: 1.92m (6ft 3.5in)
Axle Load: 14,772kg (32,500lb)
Fuel: 4,091kg (9,000lb)
Grate Area: 3m² (32sq ft)
Water: 14,982kg (3,300gal) (4,000 US gal)
Heating Surface: 166.6m² (1,793sq ft)
Superheater: Fitted later
Steam Pressure: 14kg/cm² (200psi)
Adhesive Weight: 44,545kg (98,000lb)

History: This back-to-front locomotive was designed in Florence by Giuseppe Zara of the Rete Adriatica with the driver's cab positioned at the very front, affording an excellent view and also out of the way of the exhaust smoke. Forty-three of these cab-forward Class 500 compound locomotives were built, and they remained in service for over forty years. When the Italian Railways were nationalized in 1905, they were renumbered 670.001-670.043 and, when rebuilt for superheating, were again reclassified as Class 671. The original locomotives, with the boiler and cylinders reversed on the frames, had the firebox above the bogie and the tender with water only hauled behind the chimney. Walschaert's valve gear was used, together with the Plancher system of compounding.

CLAUD HAMILTON CLASS 4-4-0

Country of Origin: Great Britain
Railway: Great Eastern Railway

Date: 1900
Length Overall: 16,276m (53ft 4.75in)
Total Weight: 96,818kg (213,000lb)
Cylinders: 2 483 × 660mm (19 × 26in)
Driving Wheels: 2.134m (7ft)
Axle Load: 18,636kg (41,000lbs)
Fuel: 3,246lit (715gal) (860 US gal) oil
Grate Area: 2m² (21.3 sq ft)
Water: 15,663lit (3,450gal) (4,150 US gal)
Heating Surface: 151m² (1,631sq ft)
Steam Pressure: 12.7kg/cm² (180psi)
Adhesive Weight: 37,272kg (82,000lbs)
Tractive Effort: 7,757kg (17,100lbs)
History: No less than 121 Claud Hamilton Class loco-
motives were originally built between 1900 and 1923
(with rebuilds being carried out until 1933). On 1

January 1948, nationalization day, 117 were still operative, with the last disappearing from service in 1958. The original batch of engines featured large cabs with four big side windows, and incorporated power-operated reversing gear and water scoop, an exhaust steam injector, and a blastpipe with variable surface. The original pre-First World War engines sported a magnificent livery of polished metal and royal blue. Two Royal Claud engines, specially painted but with green replacing the blue, were used from London to Wolferton, the station that serviced the royal home at Sandringham, until the Second World War, although the 4-4-0s had been replaced as early as 1913 by 4-6-0s for the major duties in East Anglia. The original Claud Hamiltons had pulled the 14 car Norfolk Court Express a total of 209km (130mls) in a scheduled 159 minutes.

CLASS Q 4-6-2

Country of Origin: New Zealand
Railway: New Zealand Government Railways (NZGR)
Date: 1901
Length Overall: 16.872m (55ft 4.5in)
Total Weight: 75,000kg (165,000lb)
Cylinders: 2 406 × 559mm (16 × 22in)
Driving Wheels: 1.245m (4ft 1in)
Axle Load: 10,681kg (23,500lb)
Fuel: 5,000kg (11,000lb)
Grate Area: 3.72m² (40sq ft)
Water: 7,718lit (1,700gal) (2,000 US gal)
Heating Surface: 155m² (1,673sq ft)
Steam Pressure: 14kg/cm² (200psi)
Adhesive Weight: 31,591kg (69,500lb)
Tractive Effort: 8,863kg (19,540lb)

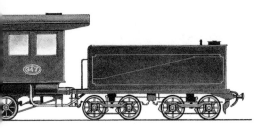

History: The world's first class of Pacific locomotive, built by Balding in the USA, 13 were shipped to New Zealand to fulfill a requirement of NZGR's Chief Mechanical Engineer, A.W. Beattie. They incorporated a large firebox capable of burning poor-quality lignite coal from the mines at Otago, South Island. The locomotives remained in operation until 1957, mostly in South Island, although some were despatched to North Island to haul the Rotorua Express between Auckland and the Rotorua hot springs. The most important technological feature of the Class Q locomotive was the Walschaert's valve gear. Located outside the frames for easy maintenance, the simplistic gear gave excellent steam distribution.

DE GLEHN ATLANTIC 4-4-2

Country of Origin: France
Railway: Northern Railway
Date: 1901
Length Overall: 18.247m (59ft 10.5in)
Total Weight: 120,227kg (264,500lb)
Cylinders: HP: 2 340 × 640mm (13.5 × 25.25in); LP: 2
560 × 640mm (22 × 25.25in)
Driving Wheels: 2.04m (6ft 8.25in)
Axle Load: 17,832kg (39,231lbs)
Fuel: 6,818kg (15,000lb)
Grate Area: 2.75m² (33.4 sq ft)
Water: 23,017lit (5,070gal) (6,080 US gal)
Heating Surface: 138m² (1,485sq ft)
Superheater: 39m² (420sq ft)
Steam Pressure: 16kg/cm² (228 psi)
Adhesive Weight: 35,681kg (78,500lbs)

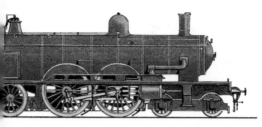

History: 152 de Glehn Atlantics were built, and in addition to the four French lines, Eastern, Paris-Orléans, Midi and the French State Railway, they were successfully exported to Great Britain, Prussia, Egypt and the USA. Englishman de Glehn rose to be Director of Engineering of the Société Alsacienne de Constructions Mécaniques at Mulhouse. His system of compounding for steam locomotives was developed with Gaston du Bousquet of the Northern Railway. A complicated system, it involved two throttles and two sets of reversing gears, together with intercepting valves. The hard-working de Glehn Atlantics provided excellent fuel efficiency and produced more power. The LP cylinders placed inside, in line with the front bogie wheels, drove the leading coupled axle; and the two outside HP cylinders, placed above the rear bogie wheels, drove the rear pair of coupled wheels.

LARGE ATLANTIC CLASS 4-4-2

Country of Origin: Great Britain
Railway: Great Northern Railway (GNR)
Date: 1902
Length Overall: 17.634m (57ft 10.25in)
Total Weight: 114,772kg (252,500lb)
Cylinders: 2 508 × 610mm (20 × 24in)
Driving Wheels: 2.032m (6ft 8in)
Axle Load: 20,454kg (45,000lbs)
Fuel: 65,909kg (14,500lb)
Grate Area: 2.88m² (31sq ft)
Water: 15,890lit (3,500gal) (4,000 US gal)
Heating Surface: 182.5m² (1,965sq ft)
Superheater: 52.8m² (568sq ft)
Steam Pressure: 12.0kg/cm² (170psi)

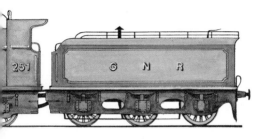

Adhesive Weight: 40,909kg (90,000lb)

Tractive Effort: 7,865kg (17,340lb)

History: Built at GNR's Doncaster plant to a design specification of Henry Ivatt, the first 81 of the 94 Large Atlantics built up to 1910 were without superheaters. The last 10 to be built had piston valves in place of the balanced slide valves and superheaters. Responsible for the introduction of the big boiler and large firebox into Great Britain, the first of these 4-4-2s remained in service until 1943, and the last-built until 1950, when in November she attained a speed of 121 km/h (75mph) on her last run. Originally costing as little as £3,400, they ran between London Kings Cross and York until superseded in 1921 by 4-6-2s.

MIDLAND COMPOUND 4-4-0

Country of Origin: Great Britain
Railway: Midland Railway (MR)

Date: 1902
Length Overall: 17.26m (56ft 7.5in)
Total Weight: 106,363kg (234,000lb)
Cylinders: HP: 1 483 × 660mm (19 × 26in); LP: 2 533 × 660mm (21 × 26in)
Driving Wheels: 2.134m (7ft)
Axle Load: 20,227kg (44,500lb)
Fuel: 5,682kg (12.500lb)
Grate Area: 2.63m² (28.4sq ft)
Water: 15,890lit (3,500gal) (4,200 US gal)
Heating Surface: 122.5m² (1,317sq ft)
Superheater: 25.3m² (272sq ft)
Steam Pressure: 14.1 kg/cm² (200 psi)
Adhesive Weight: 40,454kg (89,000lb)

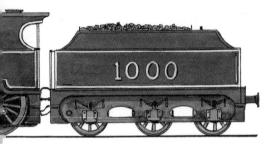

History: Regarded as the only long-term compound to be successful in Great Britain, the Midland Compound 4-4-0 was chosen as the standard express locomotive of the London Midland & Scottish Railway on its formation in 1923. Having been originally introduced by S.W. Johnson in 1902, they were developed and rebuilt by Henry Fowler in 1914, and in total 240 were built. They had a single high-pressure cylinder placed between the frames, and two low-pressure cylinders outside. The majority of Midland compounds were built at the Midland's Derby works and were nicknamed the 'Crimson Ramblers'. They employed three sets of Stephenson valve gears between the frames.

SAINT CLASS 4-6-0

Country of Origin: Great Britain
Railway: Great Western Railway (GWR)
Date: 1902
Length Overall: 19.209m (63ft 0.25in)
Total Weight: 114,090kg (251,000lb)
Cylinders: 2 470 × 762mm (18.5 × 30in)
Driving Wheels: 2.045m (6ft 8.5in)
Axle Load: 18,863kg (41,500lb)
Fuel: 6,136kg (13,500lb)
Grate Area: 2.52m² (27.1sq ft)
Water: 15,890lit (3,500gal) (4,200 US gal)
Heating Surface: 171m² (1,841sq ft)
Superheater: 24.4m² (263sq ft)
Steam Pressure: 15.8kg/cm² (225psi)
Adhesive Weight: 56,818kg (125,000lb)
Tractive Effort: 11,066kg (24,395lb)

History: The first production batch of 19 appeared in 1905, following 3 prototypes, including the original 1902 *William Dean*. Named after characters in Sir Walter Scott's Waverley novels, they preceded a batch of 10 built in 1906, which were all named after Ladies and included the first British locomotive to incorporate a modern superheater, the *Lady Superior*. 20 genuine Saints then followed in 1907, prior to a final batch of 25 superheated Courts which appeared in 1911. All Saint Class locomotives were fitted with a boiler designed by GWR's Chief Locomotive Engineer, George Jackson Churchward, which featured non-return feed valves on top of the boiler that fed the water forward, filtering out impurities as it was heated before being mixed with the water already in the boilers. In 1925, 1.828m (6ft 0in) driving wheels were fitted to the *Saint Martin* and the Hall class was born, of which 330 examples were built.

CITY CLASS 4-4-0

Country of Origin: Great Britain
Railway: Great Western Railway (GWR)
Date: 1903

Length Overall: 17.126m (56ft 2.25in)
Total Weight: 94,091kg (207,000lb)
Cylinders: 2 457 × 660mm (18 × 26in)
Driving Wheels: 2.045m (6ft 8.5in)
Axle Load: 18,636kg (41,000lb)
Fuel: 5,000kg (11,000lb)
Grate Area: 1.91m² (20.56sq ft)
Water: 13,630lit (3,000gal) (3,600 US gal)
Heating surface: 126m² (1,351sq ft)
Superheater: 20.1m² (216sq ft)
Steam Pressure: 14.1kg/cm² (200psi)
Adhesive Weight: 36,818kg (81,000lb)
Tractive Effort: 8,086kg (17,790lb)

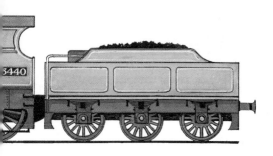

History: Only 10 true City class locomotives were built at the GWR Swindon works, although another 24 were developed from rebuilt Badminton and Atbara Class locos. In May 1905, *City of Truro*, No. 3717, while pulling a special mail train from Plymouth to Paddington, recorded a speed of 164km/h (102mph) near Taunton, Somerset – a world steam record. The City Class 4-4-0s were only ever regarded as stop-gap locomotives by GWR and were withdrawn from service in 1931. They had inside cylinders and outside cranks. The *City of Truro* is preserved in the Great Western Railway Museum at Swindon, Wiltshire, England.

CLASS P8 4-6-0

Country of Origin: Germany
Railway: Royal Prussian Union Railway (KPEV)
Date: 1906
Length Overall: 18.592m (61ft)
Total Weight: 78,409kg (172,500lb)
Cylinders: 2 575 × 630mm (22.6 × 24.8in)
Driving Wheels: 1.75m (5ft 9in)
Axle Load: 17,727kg (39,000lb)
Fuel: 5,000kg (11,000lb)
Grate Area: 2.58m² (27.8sq ft)
Water: 21,338lit (4,700gal) (5,700 US gal)
Heating Surface: 143.3m² (1,542sq ft)
Superheater: 58.9m² (634sq ft)
Steam Pressure: 12kg/cm² (170.6psi)
Adhesive Weight: 51,818kg (114,000lb)
Tractive Effort: 12,140kg (26,760lb)

History: Originally designed for express passenger work on hilly sections of the KPEV, the initial Class P8s proved unreliable and unpopular. Numerous adjustments involving the cylinder diameter and the weight distribution did nothing to improve the performance of the engine at speed, and it was thus demoted to mixed traffic work. It eventually became the most widely used and popular engine throughout Europe, with 2,350 being built for KPEV by World War I; by 1928, when production ceased, just under 4,000 had been built, including those built outside Germany. The P8s were simple and beautifully proportioned, with round-topped boilers, long narrow fireboxes, and superheaters with long-travel piston-valves. They were amongst the most efficient locomotives ever produced.

CARDEAN CLASS 4-6-0

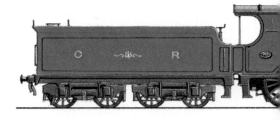

Country of Origin: Great Britain
Railway: Caledonian Railway (CR)
Date: 1906
Length Overall: 19.964m (65ft 6in)
Total Weight: 133,636kg (294,000lb)
Cylinders: 2 527 × 660mm (20.75 × 26in)
Driving Wheels: 1.981m (6ft 6in)
Axle Load: 18,863kg (41,500lb)
Fuel: 5,000kg (11,000lb)
Grate Area: 2.4m² (26sq ft)
Water: 22,700lit (5,000gal) (6,000 US gal)
Heating Surface: 168.5m² (1,814sq ft)
Superheater: 48m² (516sq ft)
Steam Pressure: 14.1kg/cm² (200psi)
Adhesive Weight: 55,909kg (123,000lb)
Tractive Effort: 10,282kg (22,667lb)

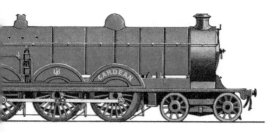

History: Only five Cardean Class 4-6-0 locomotives were built, and all at Caledonian Railway's own St Rollox works in 1906. Of these none survive, and the only Cardean to be named was the first to enter service and the last to be withdrawn from LMS as No. 14752 in 1930. The *Cardean* was allocated one train and one driver at a time, and this meant the attention she received from her proud custodians kept her in pristine condition for the 14.00hrs daily run from Glasgow to Carlisle, returning again in the evening as she took over the Euston-Glasgow train. Designed by John Farquharson McIntosh, she featured inside cylinders and Stephenson's valve gear which drove slide-valves sited on top of the cylinders via rocking levers. Superheaters were added in 1911, and eventually vacuum-break equipment.

CLASS P 4-4-2
Country of Origin: Denmark
Railway: Danish State Railways (DSB)
Date: 1907
Length Overall: 18.515m (60ft 9in)
Total Weight: 119,318kg (262,500lb)

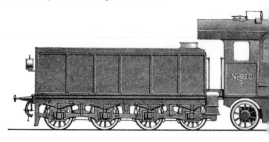

Cylinders: HP: 2 360 × 600mm (14.25 × 23.5in); LP: 2
600 × 600mm (23.5 × 23.5in)
Driving Wheels: 1.980m (6ft 6in)
Axle Load: 18,181kg (40,000lb)
Fuel: 6,136kg (13,500lb)
Grate Area: 3.2m² (34.5sq ft)
Water: 21,111lit (4,650gal) (5,550 US gal)
Heating Surface: 192.5m² (2,072psi)
Steam Pressure: 13kg/cm² (785psi)
Adhesive Weight: 36,363kg (80,000lb)

History: Nineteen Class P locomotives were built for the Danish State Railways in Hanover, Germany, by Maschinenbau. These were followed in 1910 by a further batch of 14 locomotives built in Berlin with longer cylinders and designated Class P-2. The last Class P remained in service until 1968 and is now preserved and exhibited at the Odense National Railway Museum. Walschaert's valve gear was used inside the frames, and all four cylinders drove on the rear axle.

4500 CLASS 4-6-2

Country of Origin: France
Railway: Paris-Orléans Railway (P-O)
Date: 1907
Length Overall: 20.79m (68ft 2.5in)

Total Weight: 136,818kg (301,000lb)
Cylinders: HP: 2 420 × 650mm (16.5 × 25.6in); LP: 2 640 × 650mm (25.2 × 25.6in)
Driving Wheels: 1.90m (6ft 2.75in)
Axle Load: 17,727kg (39,000lb)
Fuel: 6,136kg (13,500lb)
Grate Area: 4.27m² (46sq ft)
Water: 19,976lit (4,400gal) (5,280 US gal)
Heating Surface: 195m² (2,100sq ft)
Superheater: 63.5m² (684sq ft)
Steam Pressure: 16kg/cm² (232psi)
Adhesive Weight: 53,181kg (117,000lb)
History: One hundred 4500 Class, four cylinders, de Glehn compound locomotives were built at a rate of

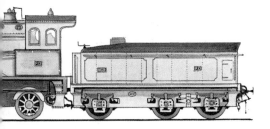

three per month. This complicated engine became the first Pacific to enter service in Europe. Built with piston valves on the high-pressure cylinders and balanced slide valves on the two low-pressure cylinders, the locomotives did not impress. The introduction of heavier steel carriages in the 1920s only added to the dissatisfaction with their performance. Replacement engines were desperately needed, but lack of financial reserves meant that the only alternative was a rebuilding programme. Enter André Chapelon, the young development engineer of the P-O, who somehow persuaded the railway to accept his drastic rebuilding proposals. The Chapelon miracle, which virtually doubled the locomotive's cylinder horsepower, created the most powerful, most efficient 4-6-2 ever built. When in 1929 No. 3566 re-entered service, reports of its feats caused a sensation throughout the world.

CLASS S 3/6 4-6-2

Country of Origin: Germany
Railway: Royal Bavarian State Railway (KBStB)
Date: 1908
Length Overall: 21.317m (69ft 11in)
Total Weight: 149,318kg (328,500lb)
Cylinders: HP: 2 425 × 610mm (16.7 × 24.0in); LP: 2 650 × 670mm (25.6 × 26.4in)
Driving Wheels: 1.87m (6ft 1.6in)
Axle Load: 17,954kg (39,500lb)
Fuel: 8,545kg (18,800lb)
Grate Area: 4.5m² (48.8sq ft)
Water: 27,376lit (6,030gal) (7,240 US gal)
Heating Surface: 197.4m² (2,125sq ft)
Superheater: 74.2m² (798sq ft)

Steam Pressure: 16kg/cm² (228psi)
Adhesive Weight: 52,727kg (116,000lb)
History: Designed by A.G. Maffei and built over a period of 23 years, the Class S 3/6 4-6-2s became famous for their work pulling the Rheingold Express both before and after World War II, remaining in service until 1966. Produced in batches, they were all classified S 3/6 but were constantly being modified, the above specification details referring to 78 engines produced between 1913 and 1924. Engines were also supplied to the Baden Railway prior to the First World War, after which 16 engines went to France and 3 to Belgium before the German State Railway reordered further locomotives in 1925.

NO. 9 4-6-0

Country of Origin: USA
Railway: Nevada-California-Oregon Railroad (NCO)

Date: 1909
Length Overall: 16.433m (53ft 11in)
Total Weight: 75,068kg (165,150lb)
Cylinders: 2 406 × 508mm (16 × 10in)
Driving Wheels: 1.117m (3ft 8in)
Axle Load: 10,893kg (23,966lb)
Fuel: 9,087lit (2,000gal) (2,400 US gal) oil
Water: 18,931lit (4,167gal) (5,000 US gal)
Steam Pressure: 12.7kg/cm² (180psi)
Adhesive Weight: 29,709kg (65,360lb)
Tractive Effort: 8,076kg (17,800lb)

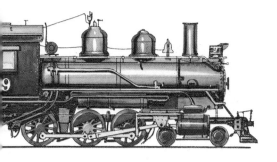

History: Built by Baldwin, these small oil-burners, of which only four were built, plied the 378km (235mls) of Nevada-California-Oregon Railroad's 914mm (3ft 0in) narrow gauge for 15 years, before being forced off the rails by Southern Pacific when they purchased the NCO in 1926 and converted the line to standard gauge. Two of the four engines were retained by SP and transferred to the narrow gauge tracks that had once formed the Carson & Colorado Railway. By the time of their withdrawal from service in 1959, No. 8 and No. 9 had become tourist attractions.

CLASS H4 4-6-2
Country of Origin: USA

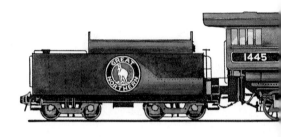

Railway: Great Northern Railway (GNR)
Date: 1909
Length Overall: 20.498m (67ft 3in)
Total Weight: 174,431kg (383,750lb)
Cylinders: 2 597 × 762mm (23.5 × 30in)
Driving Wheels: 1.854m (6ft 1in)
Axle Load: 25,181kg (55,400lb)
Fuel: 12,727kg (28,000lb)
Grate Area: 4.95m² (53.3sq ft)
Water: 30,291lit (6,667gal) (8,000 US gal)
Heating Surface: 295m² (3,177sq ft)
Superheater: 57.6m² (620sq ft)
Steam Pressure: 14.75kg/cm² (210psi)
Adhesive Weight: 68,727kg (151,200lb)

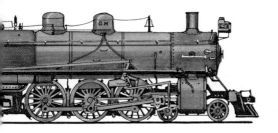

Tractive Effort: 16,193kg (35,690lb)

History: An early example of superheating, 20 H4 class Pacifics were originally purchased from Baldwin to run as the luxury Oriental Limited through from Chicago via the Burlington route to St Paul and then along the 2,926km (1,829mls) of Great Northern's own lines to Seattle, where it connected with the steamship SS *Minnesota* en route to China. Both the Great Northern and the steamship company were owned by Jerome Hill, whose self-financed railway had been built in three years, being completed on 18 September 1893. GNR purchased a further 25 Lima-built locomotives in 1913 and converted most of them to oil burning from coal burning.

FAIRLIE 0-6-6-0

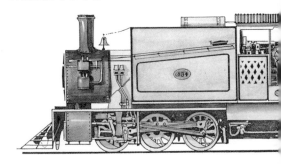

Country of Origin: Mexico
Railway: Mexican Railway (FLM)
Date: 1911
Length Overall: 15.435m (50ft 7.75in)
Total Weight: 125,454kg (276,000lb)
Cylinders: 4 483 × 635mm (19 × 25in)
Driving Wheels: 1.219m (4ft)
Axle Load: 20,909kg (46,000lb)
Fuel: 9,090kg (20,000lb)
Grate Area: 4.43m² (47.7sq ft)
Water: 15,890lit (3,500gal) (4,200 US gal)
Heating Surface: 272m² (2,924sq ft)
Steam Pressure: 12.9kg/cm² (183psi)
Adhesive Weight: 125,454kg (276,000lb)
Tractive Effort: 26,533kg (58,493lb)

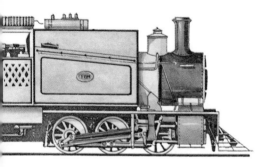

History: The Fairlie 0-6-6-0 articulated was invented by Englishman Robert Fairlie in 1864. In 1871 the British-owned Mexican Railway received its first Fairlies and they remained in service until electrification in 1923. 49 engines were delivered to Mexico in total and they were ideally suited to the 425km (264mls) of steep climbs and tight curves that constituted the very scenic route from Mexico City to Vera Cruz. The 1911 Fairlies were the most powerful British-built locomotives of the day. They employed Walschaert's valve gear with outside piston valve cylinders, a common arrangement.

CLASS S 2-6-2

Country of Origin: USSR
Railway: Ministry of Ways of Communication
Date: 1911

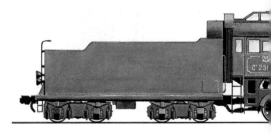

Length Overall: 23.738m (77ft 10.5in)
Total Weight: 168,409kg (370,500lb)
Cylinders: 2 575 × 700mm (22.5 × 27.5in)
Driving Wheels: 1.85m (6ft 0.75in)
Fuel: 18,181kg (40,000lb)
Grate Area: 4.72m² (51sq ft)
Water: 22,700lit (5,000gal) (6,000 US gal)
Heating Surface: 198m² (2,131sq ft)
Superheater: 89m² (958sq ft)
Steam Pressure: 13kg/cm² (185psi)
Tractive Effort: 13,653kg (30,092lb)

History. In the golden age of steam power, when Britain boasted some twenty classes of locomotives, the Soviet Union with similar lineage and traffic had just four. Of these, the most numerous (over 3,750 were built) were the S class 2-6-2s, production of which spanned forty years. Built at the Soromova works at Nizhni Novgorod (Gorki), they were very busy, simple engines with superheaters, Walschaert's valve gear and compensated springing. Some engines were later converted to oil burning.

NO.7 2-4-4T
Country of Origin: USA

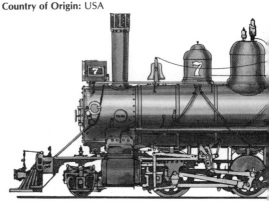

Railway: Brighton & Saco River Railroad (B&SR)
Date: 1913
Length Overall: 10.65m (34ft 7.75in)
Total Weight: 31,681kg (69,700lb)
Cylinders: 2 304 × 406mm (12 × 16in)
Driving Wheels: 0.889m (2ft 11in)
Axle Load: 9,700kg (21,340lb)
Fuel: 1,363kg (3,000lb)
Water: 3,786lit (833gal) (1,000 US gal)
Steam Pressure: 12.7kg/cm² (180psi)
Adhesive Weight: 17,636kg (38,800lb)
Tractive Effort: 4,570kg (10,072lb)

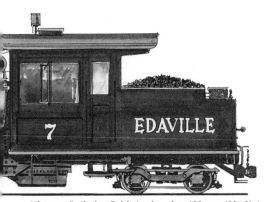

History: Built by Baldwin for the 609mm (2ft 0in) gauge B&SR, this elegant little locomotive had Walschaert's valve gear working slide valves and vacuum brakes. The engines were never overworked and were sold off in 1941 to Ellis D. Atwood, a cranberry grower from Massachusetts who built a 8.8km (5.5mls) line round his farm. Intended as farm transport, it soon became evident that demand for weekend pleasure tours would take over. Fully restored to original condition, No. 7 and sister locomotive No. 8 inaugurated the first pleasure railway in the world, the Ellis D. Atwood Railroad, on 7 April 1947.

REMEMBRANCE CLASS 4-6-4 TANK

Country of Origin: Great Britain
Railway: London, Brighton & South Coast Railway (LBSCR)
Date: 1914

Length Overall: 15.361m (50ft 475in)
Total Weight: 100,909kg (222,000lb)
Cylinders: 2 559 × 711mm (22 × 28in)
Driving Wheels: 2.057m (6ft 9in)
Axle Load: 20,000kg (44,000lb)
Fuel: 3,636kg (8,000lb)
Grate Area: 2.48m² (26.7sq ft)
Water: 12,258lit (2,700gal) (3,250 US gal)
Heating Surface: 167.7m² (1,816sq ft)
Superheater: 35.6m² (383sq ft)
Steam Pressure: 11.9kg/cm² (170psi)
Adhesive Weight: 57,272kg (126,000lb)
Tractive Effort: 10,991kg (24,180lb)

History: Produced to take the all-Pullman Southern Belle express from London to Brighton, the Remembrance Class 4-6-4s had outside Walschaert's valve gear working inside piston valves positioned between the frames, the cylinders themselves being inside the frames. Obtaining constant speeds of 120km (75mph), they remained in service with the LBSCR prestige route until 1933, when they were replaced by the electrically driven Brighton Belles. Converted to 4-6-0s in 1933 and redesignated Class N15X, the engines remained in service with British Railways until the last was withdrawn from service in 1957.

K4 CLASS 4-6-2

Country of Origin: USA

Railway: Pennsylvania Railroad (PRR)
Date: 1914
Length Overall: 25.451m (83ft 6in)
Total Weight: 242,272kg (533,000lb)
Cylinders: 2 686 × 711mm (27 × 28in)
Driving Wheels: 2.032m (6ft 8in)
Axle Load: 32,727kg (72,000lb)
Fuel: 16,363kg (36,000lb)
Grate Area: 6.5m² (70sq ft)
Water: 45,400lit (10,000gal) (12,000 US gal)
Heating Surface: 375m² (4,040sq ft)
Superheater: 88m² (943sq ft)
Steam Pressure: 14.4kg/cm² (205psi)
Adhesive Weight: 95,454kg (210,000lb)
Tractive Effort: 20,170kg (44,460lb)

History: The 425 K4 Class 4-6-2s were the mainstay of the Pennsylvania Railroad until the mid-1940s. They followed the smaller K2s, which had entered service only 4 years earlier. With the exception of a batch of 75 built by Baldwin in 1927, all K4s were built at PRR's workshops at Altoona, Pennsylvania, with the last, No. 5499, being delivered in 1928. Altoona was the only fully equipped test bed in North America where steam engines could be run up to full speed on rollers, with instrumentation checking for any faults which could then be rectified in future production engines. Economical in use, the K4s were used on all PRR's express passenger trains and were often seen crossing the Allegheny mountains with three or even four locomotives heading the train.

800 2-10-10-2

Country of Origin: USA
Railway: Virginian Railroad (VGN)
Date: 1918
Length Overall: 30.368m (99ft 8in)

Total Weight: 408,181kg (898,000lb)
Cylinders: HP: 2 762 × 872mm (30 × 32in); LP: 2 1,219 × 812mm (48 × 32in)
Driving Wheels: 1.422m (4ft 8in)
Axle Load: 28,045kg (61,700lb)
Fuel: 10,909kg (24,000lb)
Grate Area: 10.1m² (108.7sq ft)
Water: 49,070lit (10,800gal) (13,000 US gal)
Heating Surface: 799m² (8,605sq ft)
Superheater: 197m² (2,120sq ft)
Steam Pressure: 15.1kg/cm² (215psi)
Adhesive Weight: 280,454kg (617,000lb)
Tractive Effort: 80,127kg (176,600lb)

History: These 30m, 400-tonne giants were built by the American Locomotive Co. for the VGN to haul massive 5,500 tonne coal trains from Elmore, West Virginia, to Norfolk. These slow-moving monsters with 20 driving wheels served admirably for 30 years, their greatest task being the 1-in-47 incline to Clark's Gap summit, attained at a speed of 9km/h (5.5mph) with one 800 hauling and two pushing from the rear' a truly unbelievable sight. The 800s were fitted with conventional piston valves to the high-pressure cylinders, and slide valves to the two large, low pressure ones (which at 1.22m/4ft diameter were the largest ever fitted to a locomotive).

NO. 24 2-6-2
Country of Origin: USA

Railway: Sandy River & Rangeley Lakes Railroad (SRRL)
Date: 1919
Length Overall: 13.589m (44ft 7in)
Total Weight: 41,363kg (91,000lb)
Cylinders: 2 304 × 406mm (12 × 16in)
Driving Wheels: 0.838m (2ft 11in)
Axle Load: 2,454kg (5,400lb)
Fuel: 2,727kg (6,000lb)
Water: 7,572lit (1,667gal) (2,000 US gal)
Steam Pressure: 12.0kg/cm² (170psi)
Adhesive Weight: 19,091kg (42,000lb)

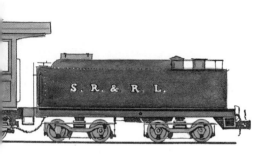

Tractive Effort: 4,576kg (10,085lb)

History: The Sandy River & Rangeley Lakes Railroad was an amalgamation of four of the seven 609mm (2ft 0in) narrow-gauge railways operating in Maine at the turn of the century. The SRRL consisted of 170km (106mls) of main line and branches, and operated 16 locomotives. It remained in business until 1936, when the line was sold for scrap. Built by Baldwin, No. 24 2-6-2 had a rather excessive 2.13m (7ft) wide tender but, apart from this feature, the engines were simple but sturdy with Walschaert's valve gear and slide valves.

CLASS A1 4-6-2

Country of Origin: Great Britain
Railway: London & North Eastern Railway (LNER)
Date: 1922
Length Overall: 21.46m (70ft 5in)
Total Weight: 150,909kg (332,000lb)
Cylinders: 3 508 × 660mm (20 × 26in)
Driving Wheels: 2.032m (6ft 8in)
Axle Load: 20,454kg (45,000lb)
Fuel: 8,181kg (18,000lb)
Grate Area: 3.8m² (41,25sq ft)
Water: 22,700lit (5,000gal) (6,000 US gal)
Heating Surface: 272m² (2,930sq ft)
Superheater: 49m² (525sq ft)
Steam Pressure: 12.6kg/cm² (180psi)
Adhesive Weight: 61,136kg (134,500lb)
Tractive Effort: 13;333kg (29,385lb)

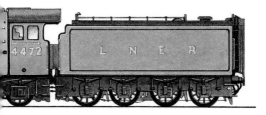

History: The first Pacific locomotives to enter service in Great Britain were Gresley's Class A1 4-6-2s and they remained a prestige passenger service until December 1965 when the last engine, British Railways No. 60041 *Salmon Trout*, was withdrawn. Problematical when introduced, alterations were made to the motion in 1926 as the result of industrial espionage carried out against Great Western Railway's Castle Class. The resultant 20% in coal savings enabled the A1s to make the longest non-stop journeys in the world from London to Edinburgh, a distance of 632km (392.75mls), with the Flying Scotsman train. In 1935, on a journey from Newcastle to London, No. 2750 *Papyrus* recorded a speed of 174km/h (108mph), the world record for an unstreamlined steam locomotive. No. 4472, the famous *Flying Scotsman*, is preserved at Steamtown Museum, Carnforth.

CASTLE CLASS 4-6-0

Country of Origin: Great Britain
Railway: Great Western Railway (GWR)
Date: 1923
Length Overall: 19.863m (65ft 2in)
Total Weight: 128,863kg (283,500lb)
Cylinders: 4 406 × 660mm (16 × 26in)
Driving Wheels: 2.045m (6ft 8.5in)
Axle Load: 20,227kg (44,500lb)
Fuel: 6,136kg (13,500lb)
Grate Area: 2.81m² (30.3sq ft)
Water: 18,160lit (4,000gal) (4,800 US gal)
Heating Surface: 190m² (2,049sq ft)
Superheater: 24.4m² (263sq ft)
Steam Pressure: 15.8kg/cm² (225psi)
Adhesive Weight: 60,681kg (133,500lb)
Tractive Effort: 14,182kg (31,625lb)

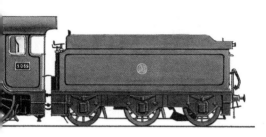

History: Charles Collett, who succeeded Churchward as Chief Mechanical Engineer at the GWR, instigated the Castle Class based on a Star Class with a newly-designed, larger boiler. The first engine, No. 4073 *Caerphilly Castle*, entered service in August 1923. This was followed by a further 170 Castles, including 15 converted Stars, which were built over a period of 27 years. When introduced, the Castle Class was the most powerful British locomotive, and for a time it held the world speed record for steam locomotives with an average speed of 131.5km/h (81.7mph) over a 124km (77.25mls) distance, achieved in 1932. The last Castle was withdrawn from service in July 1965. Seven engines have been preserved, including the first *Caerphilly Castle* at the Science Museum, London, and three of the seven are in working order.

K-36 2-8-2

Country of Origin: USA
Railway: Denver & Rio Grande Western Railroad (D&RGW)
Date: 1925
Length Overall: 20.802m (68ft 3in)
Total Weight: 130,227kg (286,500lb)
Cylinders: 2 508 × 609mm (20 × 24in)
Driving Wheels: 1.117m (3ft 8in)
Axle Load: 17,980kg (39,558lb)
Fuel: 7,272kg (16,000lb)
Grate Area: 3.7m² (40sq ft)
Water: 18,931lit (4,166gal) (5,000 US gal)
Heating Surface: 196m² (2,107sq ft)
Superheater: 53m² (575sq ft)
Steam Pressure: 13.7kg/cm² (195psi)
Adhesive Weight: 65,386kg (143,850lb)
Tractive Effort: 16,425kg (36,200lb)

History: 103km (64mls) of the Denver and Rio Grande Western Railroad were purchased in 1968 by the States of Colorado and New Mexico to run as a tourist railway, renamed the Cumbres & Toltec Scenic Railroad. They also purchased nine narrow-gauge 914mm (3ft 0in) K-36 and K-37 2-8-2s, together with over 100 assorted cars. The D&RGW was the last real steam railway in operation and at its peak comprised some 400km (250mls) of track that traversed deserts and trestle bridges, balloon loops, 1-in-25 gradients and timber-lined tunnels. Baldwin supplied ten K-36 locomotives, of which seven still survive.

P-1 4-6-4

Country of Origin: USA
Railway: Wabash Railroad (WAB)

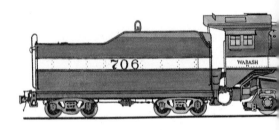

Date: 1943
Length Overall: 26.64m (87ft 5in)
Total Weight: 264,850kg (582,680lb)
Cylinders: 2 660 × 711mm (2ft 2in × 2ft 4in)
Driving Wheels: 2.03m (6ft 8in)
Axle Load: 32,727kg (72,000lb)
Fuel: 17,272kg (38,000lb)
Grate Area: 5.5m² (59sq ft)
Water: 37,868lit (8.333gal) (10,000 US gal)
Heating Surface: 393m² (4,225sq ft)
Superheater: 98m² (1,051sq ft)
Steam Pressure: 15.5kg/cm² (220psi)
Adhesive Weight: 543,800kg (1,196,360lb)

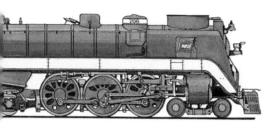

Tractive Effort: 20,074kg (44,244lb)

History: These six Class P-1 locomotives were the only 4-6-4s of the Wabash Railroad and were the result of drastic rebuilding at Wabash's own locomotive works at Decature, Illinois, of five 1925 K-5 Class 2-8-2s and one K-4 Class locomotives originally built by Alco. In the rebuilding, two cylinders replaced three, larger driving wheels were employed, roller bearings were used, and three main axles and two rear truck axles introduced. The P-1s were also streamlined to a limited degree and hauled the Wabash Express passenger trains Blue Bird and Banner Blue between St Louis and Chicago.

KING ARTHUR CLASS 4-6-0

Country of Origin: Great Britain
Railway: Southern Railway (SR)

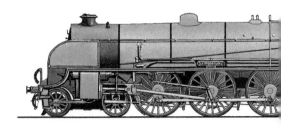

Date: 1925
Length Overall: 20.244m (66ft 5in)
Total Weight: 141,136kg (310,500lb)
Cylinders: 2 521 × 711mm (20.5 × 28in)
Driving Wheels: 2.007m (6ft 7in)
Axle Load: 20,454kg (45,000lb)
Fuel: 5,000kg (11,000lb)
Grate Area: 2.8m² (30sq ft)
Water: 22,700lit (5,000gal) (6,000 US gal)
Heating Surface: 174.5m² (1,878sq ft)
Superheater: 31.3m² (337sq ft)
Steam Pressure: 14.1kg/cm² (200psi)
Adhesive Weight: 61,136kg (134,500lb)
Tractive Effort: 11,485kg (25,320lb)

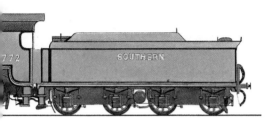

History: A total of 74 King Arthur Class 4-6-0s were built at the LSWR works, Eastleigh (44), and at the North British Locomotive Co. of Glasgow (30). They were employed on all the principal Southern Railway routes until replaced by the Lord Nelson Class in 1927. Designed by Richard Maunsell, Chief Mechanical Engineer of the newly formed Southern Railway, the 4-6-0s were basically improved N15 Class 4-6-0s, having the attributes of the 4-4-0 E1 Class incorporated, with improved combustion derived from larger ashpans and large superheaters. The National Railway Museum, York, have recently restored the first of the Class, No. *777 King Arthur*, to running order.

CLASS 01 4-6-2
Country of Origin: Germany

Railway: German State Railway (DR)
Date: 1926
Length Overall: 23.94m (78ft 6in)
Total Weight: 109,090kg (240,000lb) excluding tender
Cylinders: 2 600 × 660mm (23.6 × 26.0in)
Driving Wheels: 2m (6ft 6.7in)
Axle Load: 20,227kg (44,500lb)
Fuel: 10,000kg (22,000lb)
Grate Area: 4.41m² (47.5sq ft)
Water: 34,050lit (7,500gal) (9,000 US gal)
Heating Surface: 247.3m² (2,661sq ft)
Superheater: 85.0m² (915sq ft)
Steam Pressure: 16kg/cm² (228psi)
Adhesive Weight: 59,318kg (130,500lb)
Tractive Effort: 16,160kg (35,610lb)

History: The German State Railway was established in 1922 with the Central Locomotive Design Section being controlled by an engineer, Dr R.P. Wagner. Ten engines each of two Pacific classes were originally designed and tested: a two-cylinder Class 01, and a four-cylinder compound Class 02. The compound's marginal advantage in fuel consumption was considered to be more than offset by increased maintenance costs, and thus Class 01 was adopted and 231 were built prior to World War II. Built by AEG and Borsig of Berlin, the engines had bar frames and round-topped copper fireboxes. After the War, 171 locomotives were handed over to West Germany and 70 to East Germany, with the last West German Class 01 being withdrawn from service in 1973.

9000 4-12-2

Country of Origin: USA
Railway: Union Pacific Railroad (UP)
Date: 1926
Length Overall: 31.267m (102ft 7in)

Total Weight: 35,545kg (782,000lb)
Cylinders: 2 685 × 812mm (27 × 32in); 1 685 × 787mm (27 × 31in)
Driving Wheels: 1.70m (5ft 7in)
Axle Load: 27,272kg (60,000lb)
Fuel: 19,090kg (42,000lb)
Grate Area: 10m² (108sq ft)
Water: 56,750lit (12,500gal) (15,000 US gal)
Heating Surface: 544m² (5,853sq ft)
Superheater: 238m² (2,560sq ft)
Steam Pressure: 15.5kg/cm² (220psi)
Adhesive Weight: 16,136kg (355,000lb)
Tractive Effort: 43,852kg (96,650lb)

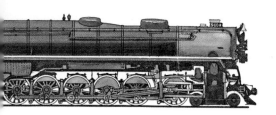

History: 88 of these enormous 12-coupled locomotives were built, and although there were other 12-coupled engines, the unique Union Pacific Railroad 9000 is the only one to be featured in this volume. They were the largest non-articulated locomotives ever built, and in order for the fixed wheel base of 9.35m (30ft 8in) to corner, the leading and trailing coupled wheels had a side play of 25mm (1in). Designed to haul the loads being handled by the Mallets, but at a higher speed and lower fuel consumption, all of the engines remained in service until the last days of steam. No. 9004 is preserved at the Transportation Museum, Los Angeles.

LORD NELSON CLASS 4-6-0

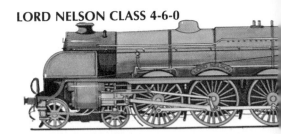

Country of Origin: Great Britain
Railway: Southern Railway (SR)
Date: 1926
Length Overall: 21.279m (69ft 9.75in)
Total Weight: 142,727kg (314,000lb)
Cylinders: 4 419 × 610mm (16.5 × 24in)
Driving Wheels: 2.007m (6ft 7in)
Axle Load: 20,909kg (46,000lb)
Fuel: 5,000kg (11,000lb)
Grate Area: 3.1m² (33sq ft)
Water: 22,700lit (5,000gal) (6,000 US gal)
Heating Surface: 185m² (1,989sq ft)
Superheater: 3.5m² (376sq ft)
Steam Pressure: 15.5kg/cm² (220psi)
Adhesive Weight: 63,181kg (139,000lb)
Tractive Effort: 15,196kg (33,500lb)

History: The more powerful replacement for the King Arthur Class appeared in 1926 in the shape of No. 850 *Lord Nelson*. Another 15 locomotives were built, seven in 1928 and eight the following year, to handle the larger loads of the holiday expresses. The Lord Nelsons were quite magnificent engines, but complex, having rather inaccessible mechanisms. They had Walschaert's valve gear between the frames, together with the four cylinders. Their biggest problem, however, was their reluctance to fire. They had a 2.74m (9ft) grate which was level at the rear, and this required not only a good knowledge of the engine but consistently accurate placing of the shovelfuls of coal, a quality not easy to develop in firemen throughout the SR network when there were only 15 Lord Nelson Class locomotives. Once running, however, they were admirable engines and the preserved Lord Nelson which is housed at the National Railway Museum, York, is regularly used for main-line excursions.

CLASS Ps-4 4-6-2

Country of Origin: USA
Railway: Southern Railway (SR)
Date: 1926
Length Overall: 28.038m (91ft 11.9in)
Total Weight: 255,454kg (562,000lb)
Cylinders: 2 686 × 711mm (27 × 28in)
Driving Wheels: 1.854m (6ft 1in)
Axle Load: 27,727kg (61,000lb)
Fuel: 14,545kg (32,000lb)
Grate Area: 6.55m² (70.5sq ft)
Water: 52,664lit (11,600gal) (14,000 US gal)
Heating Surface: 343m² (3,689sq ft)
Superheater: 92.3m² (993sq ft)
Steam Pressure: 14.1kg/cm² (200psi)
Adhesive Weight: 82,727kg (182,000lb)
Tractive Effort: 21,590kg (47,500lb)

History: 36 Class Ps-4 4-6-2s were built in 1923, based on the design of the United States Railroad Administration's 4-6-2 heavy-type locomotive used for all types of traffic. A further batch of 23 locomotives was built in 1926. These had the twelve-wheeled tenders and were painted green and gold after the British Southern Railway livery. The majority of the engines, all built by Baldwin, had Walschaert's valve gear, although some were built with Baker valve gear, and they all had mechanical stokers. A total of 64 were built and were the last steam passenger locomotives to be ordered by Southern, who kept them operational on their major passenger lines until 1940, when they were replaced by diesels. No. 1401, illustrated here, is on exhibition at the Smithsonian Museum, Washington DC.

ROYAL SCOT CLASS 4-6-0

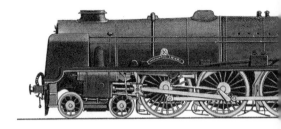

Country of Origin: Great Britain
Railway: London Midland & Scottish (LMS)
Date: 1927
Length Overall: 19.787m (64ft 11in)
Total Weight: 142,045kg (312,500lb)
Cylinders: 3 457 × 660mm (18 × 26in)
Driving Wheels: 2.057m (6ft 9in)
Axle Load: 20,909kg (46,000lb)
Fuel: 9,090kg (20,000lb)
Grate Area: 2.90m² (31.25sq ft)
Water: 18,160lit (4,000gal) (4,800 US gal)
Heating Surface: 172m² (1,851sq ft)
Superheater: 34.1m² (367sq ft)
Steam Pressure: 17.6kg/cm² (250psi)
Adhesive Weight: 62,272kg (137,000lb)
Tractive Effort: 15,037kg (33,150lb)

History: The design of the Royal Scots was as advanced as any British 4-6-0 could be in the 1920s. The impetus came from the successful work of the Launceston Castle Class with some influence of the Lord Nelson Class. The coupled wheelback broke Derby tradition, and the relatively close spacing of the last pairs of wheels led to the adoption of a stepped grate. Three-cylinder simple expression with divided drive was adopted. The single inside cylinder drove the leading axle, whilst the outside pair drove the centre wheels with three independent sets of Walschaert's valve gears, an arrangement which led to considerable advantages, making the locomotives efficient and free running. 70 Royal Scot Class locomotives were built in total with No. 6115 *Scots Guardsman* being the last to be withdrawn from service in January 1966.

159

A-6 4-4-2
Country of Origin: USA

Railway: Southern Pacific (SP)
Date: 1927
Length Overall: 23.99m (78ft 8.5in)
Total Weight: 211,772kg (465,900lb)
Cylinders: 2 558 × 711mm (22 × 28in)
Driving Wheels: 2.057m (6ft 9in)
Axle Load: 15,000kg (33,000lb)
Fuel: 11,123lit (2,450gal) (2,940 US gal) oil
Grate Area: 4.6m² (49,5sq ft)
Water: 34,050lit (7,500gal) (9,000 US gal)
Steam Pressure: 14.8kg/cm² (210psi)
Adhesive Weight: 28,181kg (62,000lb)
Tractive Effort: 18,768kg (41,360lb)

History: The last of Southern Pacific's 4-4-2s, the A-6 class locomotives were built at SP's workshops in Los Angeles and Sacramento, the initial batch of five being a virtual rebuilding of A-3 engines built by Alco and Baldwin as early as 1904. The rebuilds included the substitution of Walschaert's valve gear for Stephenson's, and the addition of a booster engine which drove the rear wheels and increased the tractive effort by more than 40 per cent. Two engines were assigned to the running of the prestigious Daylight Express train between Los Angeles and San Francisco, and were specially painted in orange and black livery for this role.

KING CLASS 4-6-0

Country of Origin: Great Britain
Railway: Great Western Railway (GWR)
Date: 1927
Length Overall: 20.777m (68ft 2in)
Total Weight: 138,181kg (304,000lb)
Cylinders: 4 413 × 711mm (16.25 × 28in)
Driving Wheels: 1.981m (6ft 6in)
Axle Load: 22,954kg (50,500lb)
Fuel: 6,136kg (13,500lb)
Grate Area: 3.19m² (343sq ft)
Water: 18,160lit (4,000gal) (4,800 US gal)
Heating Surface: 204m² (2,201sq ft)
Superheater: 29.0m² (313sq ft)
Steam Pressure: 17.6kg/cm² (250psi)
Adhesive Weight: 68,636kg (151,000lb)
Tractive Effort: 18,285kg (40,300lb)
History: The four-cylinder King Class 4-6-0s replaced
the less powerful Castles, which had in turn replaced

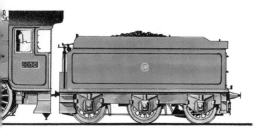

the Star Class locomotives, with each basically being a stretched version of its predecessor. Derived from the de Glehn arrangement, with the outside cylinders driving the coupled axle, and the inside pair driving the leading axle, both sets of cylinders were horizontal, with each adjacent pair being diametrically opposed. Walschaert's valve gear was used, positioned inside the frames. The first six Kings entered service in 1927 and the last of the 30-strong class in August 1930. All were withdrawn from service in 1962. The Kings were named in reverse chronological order, beginning with the current monarch King George V. The GWR's King class was its largest and most prestigious passenger locomotive. Built in a hurry in order to beat the opposition, and to meet the deadline for the Baltimore and Ohio's 'Fair of The Iron Horse', it proved to be all its builders could have wished.

AC-4 Cab Forward 4-8-8-2

Country of Origin: USA
Railway: Southern Pacific (SP)
Date: 1928
Length Overall: 38.075m (124ft 11in)
Total Weight: 477,818kg (1,051,200lb)
Cylinders: 4 .609 × .812m (2ft 0in × 2ft 8in)
Driving Wheels: 1.61m (5ft 3.5in)
Axle Load: 31,800kg (69,960lb)
Fuel: 23,076lit (5,083gal) (6,100 US gal) oil
Grate Area: 12.9m² (139sq ft)
Water: 83,232lit (18,333gal) (22,000 US gal)
Heating Surface: 601m² (6,470sq ft)
Superheater: 243m² (2,616sq ft)
Steam Pressure: 17.6kg/cm² (250psi)
Adhesive Weight: 241,682kg (531,700lb)
Tractive Effort: 56,397kg (124,300lb)

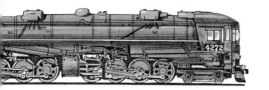

History: Southern Pacific purchased a total of 243 cab forward locomotives. The first, entering service in 1911, comprised of a batch of 12 'Mallet-Mogul' 2-6-6-2 engines. These were later corrected to 4-6-6-2s and although intended for passenger work, proved too slow and were thus relegated to freight trains. During 1912 and 1913 a further 36 were built, in three batches, with 2-8-8-2 arrangement, they were known as Mallet-Consolidations and designated MC-2, MC-4, MC-6. The first Articulated-Consolidation locomotives (AC-4s) were ordered from Baldwin in 1928 and by 1944 195 had been delivered and the earlier MC classes were converted to AC Class locomotives. These highly successful locomotives were nevertheless very slow with maximum speeds of only 89km/h (55mph).

CLASS V 4-4-0

Country of Origin: Ireland

Railway: Great Northern Railway (GNR(I))
Date: 1932
Length Overall: 16.853m (55ft 3.5in)
Total Weight: 105,454kg (232,000lb)
Cylinders: HP: 1 438 × 660mm (17.25 × 26in); LP: 2 483 × 660mm (19 × 26in)
Driving Wheels: 2.007m (6ft 7in)
Axle Load: 21,363kg (47,000lb)
Fuel: 6,000kg (13,200lb)
Grate Area: 2.3m² (25sq ft)
Water: 15,840lit (3,500gal) (4,200 US gal)
Heating Surface: 116m² (1,251sq ft)
Superheater: 25.6m² (278sq ft)
Steam Pressure: 17.6kg/cm² (250psi)
Adhesive Weight: 41,818kg (92,000lb)

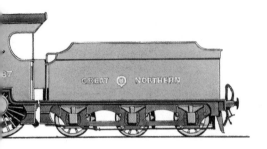

History: The Boyne River viaduct on the main Dublin to Belfast line had been a restricting factor since the railway's inauguration in 1876, but in 1931 the viaduct was strengthened and the advent of the powerful express locomotives, of which the five Class V compounds were the first, was to hand. Built by Beyer, Peacock, the locomotives featured Stephenson's link motion, and all cylinders had piston valves. The running time from Dublin to Belfast was cut to 148 minutes, including the border stop and five fuelling stops. The 4-4-0s remained in service until 1961.

SCHOOLS CLASS 4-4-0
Country of Origin: Great Britain

Railway: Southern Railway (SR)
Date: 1930
Length Overall: 17.926m (58ft 9.75in)
Total Weight: 111,591kg (245,800lb)
Cylinders: 3 419 × 660mm (16.5 × 26in)
Driving Wheels: 2.007m (6ft 7in)
Axle Load: 21,363kg (47,000lb)
Fuel: 5,000kg (11 000lb)
Grate Area: 2.63m² (28.3sq ft)
Water: 18,160lit (4,000gal) (4,800 US gal)
Heating Surface: 164m² (1,766sq ft)
Superheater: 26.3m² (283sq ft)
Steam Pressure: 15.46kg/cm² (220psi)
Adhesive Weight: 42,727kg (94,000lb)
Tractive Effort: 11,400kg (25,133lb)

History: A total of 40 Schools Class 4-4-0 locomotives were built between 1930 and 1935. All had three cylinders, all driving the leading coupled axle and each with its own Walschaert's valve gear. Shorter than the majority of their contemporaries, they proved to be highly successful and very few modifications were required over the years. First of the Class was No. 900 *Eton,* and the initial batch of ten were all built at the Eastleigh Works. No. 919 *Harrow* depicted above was from the 1933 batch and was the first to be named after a school outside the SR's territory. The Schools Class locomotives remained in service until 1962. Three have been preserved, including No. 925 *Cheltenham,* now exhibited at the National Railway Museum, York.

KF TYPE 4-8-4

Country of Origin: China
Railway: Chinese Ministry of Railways
Date: 1935

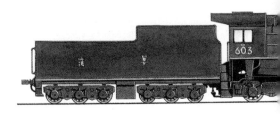

Length Overall: 28.41m (93ft 2.5in)
Total Weight: 196,363kg (432,000lb)
Cylinders: 2 540 × 750mm (21.25 × 29.5in)
Driving Wheels: 1.75m (5ft 9in)
Axle Load: 17,272kg (38,000lb)
Fuel: 12,045kg (26,500lb)
Grate Area: 6.4m² (68.5sq ft)
Water: 29.964lit (6,600gal) (8,000 US gal)
Heating Surface: 278m² (2,988sq ft)
Superheater: 100m² (1,076sq ft)
Steam Pressure: 15.5kg/cm² (220psi)
Adhesive Weight: 68,181kg (150,000lb)
Tractive Effort: 16,380kg (36,100lb)

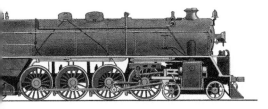

History: Featuring many little extras such as electric light, automatic stokers, and indicators for valve gear setting, these 24 British-built 4-8-4s not surprisingly proved very popular with their crews, who in looking after their charges also obtained excellent service from them. Some of the 24 locomotives also had a booster engine fitted to the leading tender bogie with drive on four wheels, and all had Walschaert's valve gear. Most survived World War II and remained in operation with both the Canton-Hanken and the Shanghai-Nanking Railways until the 1960s. In 1981 No. KF7 was donated to the National Railway Museum, York, by the Chinese People's Republic.

ANDES CLASS 2-8-0

Country of Origin: Peru
Railway: Central Railway of Peru (FCC)
Date: 1935
Length Overall: 18.879m (61ft 11.25in)
Total Weight: 113,636kg (250,000lb)

Cylinders: 2 508 × 711mm (20 × 28in)
Driving Wheels: 1.321m (4ft 4in)
Axle Load: 16,591kg (36,500lb)
Fuel: 6,656lit (1,465gal) (1,760 US gal) oil
Grate Area: 2.6m² (28sq ft)
Water: 12,031lit (2,650gal) (3,180 US gal)
Heating Surface: 160m² (1,717sq ft)
Superheater: 32m² (341sq ft)
Steam Pressure: 14.1kg/cm² (200psi)
Adhesive Weight: 66,364kg (146,000lb)
Tractive Effort: 16,600kg (36,600lb)

History: These robust little engines, built by Beyer, Peacock, were supplied to the Central Railway of Peru who worked 29 locomotives, Cerro de Pasco Railroad, five, and Southern Railway of Peru, 20. They featured a short boiler to enable them to tackle the steep gradients of the line from Lima to Galera which climbed 4,750m (15,750ft) in less than 150km (93mls). They also featured air sanding and a complicated air braking system. Because of ample water supplies only a small tender was necessary. No. 206 has been preserved at the Lima Railway Museum.

CLASS A 4-4-2

Country of Origin: USA
Railway: Chicago, Milwaukee, St Paul & Pacific Railroad (CMStP&P)
Date: 1935
Length Overall: 27.026m (88ft 8in)
Total Weight: 244,091kg (537,000lb)
Cylinders: 2 483 × 711mm (19 × 28in)
Driving Wheels: 2 134m (7ft)
Axle Load: 32,955kg (72,500lb)
Fuel: 14,982lit (3,300gal) (4,000 US gal) oil
Grate Area: 6.4m² (69sq ft)
Water: 49,032lit (10,800gal) (13,000 US gal)
Heating Surface: 301.5m² (3,245sq ft)
Superheater: 96m² (1,029sq ft)

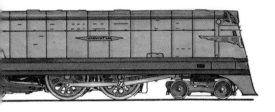

Steam Pressure: 21kg/cm² (300psi)
Adhesive Weight: 65,682kg (144,500lb)
Tractive Effort: 13,920kg (30,685lb)
History: These beautiful, brightly coloured, stream-lined locomotives were built by the American Loco-motive Company of Schenectady, New York. The first locomotives ordered and built for a daily operation at 161km/h (100mph), they were capable of developing 3,000hp and speeds of 175km/h (110mph). Only four Class A locomotives were built, two in 1935 and one each in 1936 and 1937, and they competed admirably in the competitive daily runs from Chicago to St Paul and Minneapolis, hauling the nine-car luxury Hiawatha trains.

A4 CLASS 4-6-2

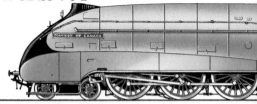

Country of Origin: Great Britain
Railway: London & North Eastern (LNER)
Date: 1935
Length Overall: 21.64m (71ft 0in)
Total Weight: 167,795kg (370,000lb)
Cylinders: (3) 470 × 660mm (18.5 × 26in)
Driving Wheels: 2,032mm (80in)
Axle Load: 22,448kg (49,500lb)
Fuel: 8,163kg (18,000lb)
Grate Area: 3.8m² (41sq ft)
Water: 22,717lit (5,000gal)
Heating Surface: 240m² (2,576sq ft)
Superheater: 70m² (749sq ft)
Steam Pressure: 17.5kg/cm² (250psi)
Adhesive Weight: 67,118kg (148,000lb)
Tractive Effort: 16,086kg (35,455lb)
History: Without doubt the Class A4 streamlined 4-6-2 is the most popular and probably the best steam locomotive ever built; it is also the holder of the world speed record for steam locomotives. A direct

decendant of the Class A1 Flying Scotsman, the A4 was designed to run between London and Newcastle, a distance of 429km (268mls). The first of four streamlined locomotives, No 2509 *Silver Link* was steamed up on 5 September 1935 and broke the speed record on its press trip on 27 September when it achieved 180km/h (112.5mph). The streamlined matching locomotive and train The Silver Jubilee entered public service on 30 September and was an immediate success. A further 31 A4's were built between 1936 and 1938 and two further streamlined trains Coronation and West Riding Limited entered service. On 4 July 1938 No 4468 *Mallard* broke the World Steam Traction Speed Record with a sustained speed of 201km/h (125mph). The original locomotives were silver painted, those in general service LNER green and those for Coronation plus Golden Fleece and Golden Shuttle for the West Riding Limited were blue, which by 1938 became the standard colour.

CLASS 05
Country of Origin: Germany

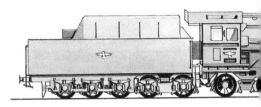

Railway: German State Railway (DR)
Date: 1935
Length Overall: 26.265m (86ft 2in)
Total Weight: 215,938kg (475,064lb)
Cylinders: 3 450 × 660mm (17.75 × 26in)
Driving Wheels: 2.3m (7ft 6.5in)
Axle Load: 19,545kg (43,000lb)
Fuel: 10,000kg (22,000lb)
Grate Area: 4.71m² (51sq ft)
Water: 37,228lit (8,200gal) (9,870 US gal)
Heating Surface: 256m² (2,750sq ft)
Superheater: 90m² (976sq ft)
Steam Pressure: 20kg/cm² (284psi)
Adhesive Weight: 57,727kg (127,000lb)
Tractive Effort: 14,870kg (32,776lb)

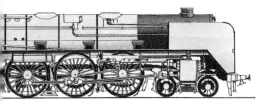

History: Entering service in October 1936 between Hamburg and Berlin, the 05 Class was designed to operate at a normal running speed of 150km/h (94mph), which was then the highest speed of any European steam train. Designed by Adolf Wolff and built by Börsig of Berlin, the partially streamlined engines incorporated large driving wheels and very large valves. A unique feature was the fitting of two braking blocks on all wheels with the exception of the leading bogie wheels. Only three engines were ever built. They were withdrawn from service during World War II, returning to operation without streamlining in 1950, and continued for another seven years. No. 05001 was restored in 1961 and is now in the Nuremberg National Railway Museum.

V2 CLASS 2-6-2

Country of Origin: Great Britain
Railway: London & North Eastern Railway (LNER)

Date: 1936
Length Overall: 20.244m (66ft 5in)
Total Weight: 146,818kg (323,000lb)
Cylinders: 3 470 × 660mm (18.5 × 26in)
Driving Wheels: 1.88m (6ft 2in)
Axle Load: 22,500kg (49,500lb)
Fuel: 7,727kg (17,000lb)
Grate Area: 3.86m² (41.25sq ft)
Water: 19,068lit (4,200gal) (5,040 US gal)
Heating Surface: 225.8m² (2,431sq ft)
Superheater: 63.2m² (680sq ft)
Steam Pressure: 15.5kg/cm² (220psi)
Adhesive Weight: 66,364kg (146,000lb)
Tractive Effort: 15,304kg (33,730lb)

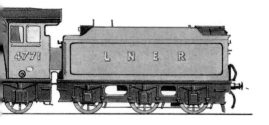

History: Originally intended for fast fitted freights, the 'Green Arrows' proved an equal match to the A3 Pacifics – a point duly recognized when they were allocated work on the Yorkshire Pullman in 1939. 184 of the Class **were** eventually built. Their enormous reputation **was ga**ined during World War II, and was built on performances such as the 26-coach load hauled by No. 4800 from Peterborough to Kings Cross in 102 minutes, a gross load of some 873,815kg (1,922,393lbs) – more than double the load for which the Class was designed. V2s remained in service until 1966. No. 4771 *Green Arrow* has been preserved in working condition in the National Railway Museum, York.

231-132BT CLASS 4-6-2 + 2-6-4

Country of Origin: Algeria
Railway: Paris, Lyons & Mediterranean Railway (PLM)

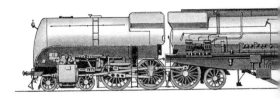

Date: 1937
Length Overall: 29.432m (96ft 6.8in)
Total Weight: 21,591kg (47,500lb)
Cylinders: 4 490 × 660mm (19.25 × 26in)
Driving Wheels: 1.8m (5ft 11in)
Axle Load: 18,409kg (40,500lb)
Fuel: 10,909kg (24,000lb)
Grate Area: 5.4m² (58sq ft)
Water: 29,964lit (6,600gal) (7,900 US gal)
Heating Surface: 260m² (2,794sq ft)
Superheater: 91m² (975sq ft)
Steam Pressure: 20kg/cm² (284psi)
Adhesive Weight: 109,545kg (241,000lb)
Tractive Effort: 29,920kg (65,960lb)

History: These Beyer-Garratts, built by Raismes in France, were designed for freight and mixed-traffic use. An initial order for 10 was placed by the Paris, Lyons & Mediterranean Company, with 19 further locomotives being ordered when the PLM amalgamated with Algerian State Railways to form Algerian Railways. A prototype had previously been built and tested in 1932. Features included electrically operated Cossart valve gear, which drove cam-operated piston valves. Duplicate controls were supplied at the rear of the cab for reverse running, and the cabs were also fitted with turbofan ventilation. The 231-132BT Class were withdrawn from service in 1957, being replaced by diesels.

ROYAL HUDSON CLASS 4-6-4

Country of Origin: Canada
Railway: Canadian Pacific Railway (CPR)
Date: 1937
Length Overall: 27.686m (90ft 10in)
Total Weight: 299,545kg (659,000lb)
Cylinders: 2 559 × 762mm (22 × 30in)
Driving Wheels: 1.905m (6ft 3in)
Axle Load: 29,545kg (65,000lb)
Fuel: 21,364kg (47,000lb)
Grate Area: 7.5m² (81sq ft)
Water: 54,480lit (12,000gal) (14,400 US gal)
Heating Surface: 352m² (3,791sq ft)
Superheater: 143m² (1,542sq ft)
Steam Pressure: 19.3kg/cm² (275psi)
Adhesive Weight: 88,162kg (194,000lb)
Tractive Effort: 20,548kg (45,300lb)

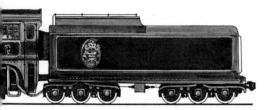

History: A total of 45 4-6-4 Royal Hudson Class locomotives were built between 1937 and 1945 and were designed to replace Canadian Pacific's leading G-3 Class express passenger locomotives. Originally designated Class H-1, they featured mechanical stokers and large superheaters with front-end throttles fitted to their sides, enabling superheated steam to be fed to auxiliary parts. In 1939 No. 2850, painted royal blue and silver and with the royal arms emblazoned on its tender, hauled the royal train of King George VI and Queen Elizabeth on their lengthy visit to Canada; from then on, a crown was painted at the front of the running board. These 4-6-4s remained in service until 1966. Five still survive, including No. 2860 which hauls tourist trains on the British Columbia Railway from Vancouver to Squamish.

CLASS J3a 4-6-4
Country of Origin: USA

Railway: New York Central Railroad (NYC)
Date: 1937
Length Overall: 32.342m (106ft 1in)
Total Weight: 354,545kg (780,000lb)
Cylinders: 2 572 × 737mm (22.5 × 29in)
Driving Wheels: 2.007m (6ft 7in)
Axle Load: 30,681kg (67,500lb)
Fuel: 41,818kg (92,000lb)
Grate Area: 7.6m² (82sq ft)
Water: 68,100lit (15,000gal) (18,000 US gal)
Heating Surface: 389m² (4,187sq ft)
Superheater: 162.1m² (1,745sq ft)
Steam Pressure: 18.6kg/cm² (265psi)
Adhesive Weight: 91,590kg (201,500lb)
Tractive Effort: 19,000kg (41,860lb)
History: The Class J3 Hudsons were the final development of the American Locomotive Company-built 4-6-4s, which had begun in 1926 with the Class J1a, the

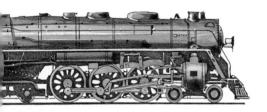

first 4-6-4 in the United States. The original Class J1a had Walschaert's valve gear; subsequent developments used Baker's gear which, because it had no moving parts, required less maintenance. The last Class J1s were built in 1932. The first 50 J3 Class locomotives incorporated various improvements such as disc driving wheels, tapered boiler barrels – which helped increase the pressure from 15.9kg/cm² (225psi) to 18.6kg/cm² (265psi) – and a 1.09m (3ft 7in) long combustion chamber in the firebox. The NYC had 275 4-6-4 locomotives, the largest fleet of such locomotives anywhere in the world. They were used to haul NYC's famous Twentieth Century Limited train from New York to Chicago in a scheduled time of 16 hours, 4 hours faster than their J1 predecessors. The J3s were replaced to some degree by the Niagara Class 4-8-4s after World War II, but some engines remained in service until 1956.

CLASS GS-2 4-8-4

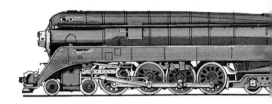

Country of Origin: USA
Railway: Southern Pacific Railroad (SP)
Date: 1937
Length Overall: 30.91m (101ft 5in)
Total Weight: 401,364kg (883,000lb)
Cylinders: 2 648 × 813mm (25.5 × 32in)
Driving Wheels: 1.87m (6ft 1.5in)
Axle Load: 31,330kg (68,925lb)
Fuel: 22,263lit (4,900gal) (5,900 US gal) oil
Grate Area: 8.4m² (90.4sq ft)
Water: 88,984lit (19,600gal) (23,500 US gal)
Heating Surface: 454m² (4,887sq ft)
Superheater: 194m² (2,086sq ft)
Steam Pressure: 21.1kg/cm² (300psi)
Adhesive Weight: 125,455kg (276,000lb)
Tractive Effort: 32,285kg (71,173lb)

History: Employed on the 750km (470mls) route between Los Angeles and San Francisco, the GS-2 streamlined locomotive pulled the Daylight Express with its 12 matching cars, serving the SP for 20 years. Built by the Lima Locomotive Works, Ohio, they featured electropneumatic braking equipment, spring-controlled sideplay on the leading coupled axle, air sanding gear, three turbo-generators, and a feedwater heater and pump in addition to injectors. Sixty locomotives were built in total; the first batch of six designated GS-2 in 1937 had smaller driving wheels. No. 4460 is preserved at the Museum of Transportation, St Louis, Missouri.

CLASS 'O' 4-6-2

Country of Origin: Malaysia
Railway: Malayan Railway (PKTM)

Date: 1938
Length Overall: 18.628m (61ft 1.4in)
Total Weight: 102,727kg (226,000lb)
Cylinders: 3 330 × 610mm (13 × 24in)
Driving Wheels: 1.372m (4ft 6in)
Axle Load: 12,982kg (28,560lb)
Fuel: 10,000kg (22,000lb)
Grate Area: 2.5m² (27sq ft)
Water: 15,890lit (3,500gal) (4,200 US gal)
Heating Surface: 103m² (1,109sq ft)
Superheater: 20.25m² (218sq ft)
Steam Pressure: 17.5kg/cm² (250psi)
Adhesive Weight: 39,091kg (86,000lb)
Tractive Effort: 10,859kg (23,940lb)

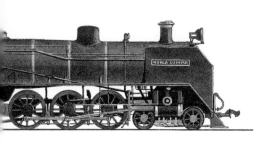

History: Built by the North British Locomotive Company, 68 of these metre-gauge locomotives were supplied to the Malaysian Railway (formerly the Federated Malaya States Railway). Originally designated Class 'O', they were re-designated after World War II as Class 56. The locomotives have Roman lettering one side of the engine and Malay script on the other. Their three cylinders all drive the middle coupled axle, and this provides smooth running over the lightly laid track on which there is a speed limit of 72.5km/h (45mph). The engines were converted to oil burning about 1955, but were replaced by diesels in 1957, the last engine being withdrawn from service in 1981.

DUCHESS CLASS 4-6-2

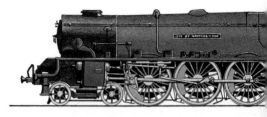

Country of Origin: Great Britain
Railway: London, Midland & Scottish Railway (LMS)
Date: 1939
Length Overall: 22.51m (73ft 10.25in)
Total Weight: 164,545kg (362,000lb)
Cylinders: 4 419 × 711mm (16.5 × 28in)
Driving Wheels: 2.057m (6ft 9in)
Axle Load: 23,864kg (52,500lb)
Fuel: 10,182kg (22,400lb)
Grate Area: 4.6m² (50sq ft)
Water: 18,160lit (4,000gal) (4,800 US gal)
Heating Surface: 261m² (2,807sq ft)
Superheater: 79.5m² (856sq ft)
Steam Pressure: 17.6kg/cm² (250psi)
Adhesive Weight: 67,045kg (147,500lb)
Tractive Effort: 18,144kg (40,000lb)

History: The Duchess Class holds the distinction of being the most powerful steam locomotive ever to be run in Great Britain. In February 1939, using two firemen, it ran from Glasgow to Crewe and recorded an indicated horse power of 3,300. Designed by William Stanier, who had joined the LMS from the GWR in 1932, the Duchess Class incorporated outside valve gear which worked the valves on both the inside and outside of the cylinders via rocker arms behind the outside cylinders. Another feature was the steam-operated coal-pusher which moved the coal forward from the back of the tender. Thirty-eight Duchess Class 4-6-2s were built, with the last being withdrawn from service in 1964. Some of the class were originally streamlined, and three have been preserved: *Duchess of Hamilton* at the National Railway Museum, York; *Duchess of Sutherland*, in Alan Bloom's Collection, Bressingham Norfolk and *City of Birmingham*, in the Birmingham Science Museum.

CLASS 12 4-4-2

Country of Origin: Belgium
Railway: Belgium National Railways (SNCB)
Date: 1939
Length Overall: 21.19m (69ft 6.25in)
Total Weight: 85,682kg (188,500lb) excluding tender
Cylinders: 2 480 × 720mm (18.8 × 28.4in)

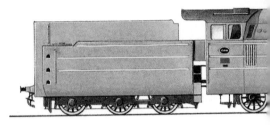

Driving Wheels: 2.1m (6ft 10.75in)
Axle Load: 23,636kg (52,000lb)
Fuel: 7,955kg (17,500lb)
Grate Area: 3.7m² (39.8sq ft)
Water: 23,971lit (5,280gal) (6,300 US gal)
Heating Surface: 161m² (1,729sq ft)
Superheater: 63m² (678sq ft)
Steam Pressure: 18kg/cm² (256psi)
Adhesive Weight: 45,909kg (101,000lb)
Tractive Effort: 12,079kg (26,620lb)

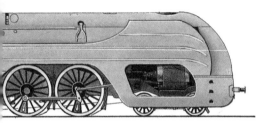

History: Designed for the 120km (75mls) Brussels to Ostend line, the Class 12 4-4-2s of the Belgium National Railways were scheduled to make the trip including a stop at Bruges in exactly one hour. These streamlined engines were the world's last 4-4-2s and were built by Cockrill in Belgium. Their operational life was extremely short as World War II broke out within a few months of their entering service in 1939. No. 1203 has been preserved by Belgium National Railways, and is on exhibition at Louvain.

CLASS J 4-8-4

Country of Origin: USA
Railway: Norfolk & Western Railway (N&W)
Date: 1941
Length Overall: 30.759m (100ft 11in)
Total Weight: 396,818kg (873,000lb)
Cylinders: 2 686 × 813mm (27 × 32in)
Driving Wheels: 1.778m (5ft 10in)
Axle Load: 32,727kg (72,000lb)
Fuel: 31,818kg (70,000lb)
Grate Area: 10m² (107.5sq ft)
Water: 75,818lit (16,700gal) (20,000 US gal)
Heating Surface: 490m² (5,271sq ft)
Superheater: 202m² (2,177sq ft)
Steam Pressure: 21kg/cm² (300psi)
Adhesive Weight: 130,909kg (288,000lb)
Tractive Effort: 36,287kg (80,000lb)

History: The Class J locomotive was designed and built by the Norfolk and Western Railway at their HQ at Roanoke, Virginia. The locomotive's frame was of cast steel, and the engine featured a multitude of bearings which were all oiled automatically from a 110lit (24gal) tank. Baker's valve gear was fitted, and together with an enormous tender the result was a locomotive that only needed to visit the workshops every 18 months, and which averaged a monthly 24,000km (15,000mls). Regular servicing for cleaning and oil change only took an hour, and all this helped to make the N&W the best organized, equipped and profitable railroad in North America by 1950. The J Class was the last express steam passenger locomotive to be built in North America and one has been restored to running order at the Roanoke Transport Museum.

BIG BOY 4-8-8-4

Country of Origin: USA
Railway: Union Pacific Railroad (UP)

Date: 1941
Length Overall: 40.487m (132ft 10in)
Total Weight: 540,682kg (1,189,500lb)
Cylinders: 4 603 × 812mm (23.75 × 32in)
Driving Wheels: 1.727m (5ft 8in)
Axle Load: 30,795kg (67,750lb)
Fuel: 25,455kg (56,000lb)
Grate Area: 13.9m² (150sq ft)
Water: 94,500lit (20,800 gal) (25,000 US gal)
Heating Surface: 547m² (5,889sq ft)
Superheater: 229m² (2,466sq ft)
Steam Pressure: 21.1kg/cm² (300psi)
Adhesive Weight: 245,455kg (540,000lb)
Tractive Effort: 61,422kg (135,375lb)

History: It was in September 1941 that the first Big Boy entered service with the Union Pacific Railroad, since when they have been acclaimed worldwide as everything that was big and powerful in US railroading. There were bigger locomotives, there were more powerful locomotives, but nothing surpasses the reputation of these four-cylinder 40m (132ft) giants. Union Pacific had to install new turntables and heavier rails to cope with them and their 6,000-ton trains which were capable of travelling at speeds of 112km/h (70mph). Cast steel frames were used, as were roller bearings, and in all 201 Big Boys were built. Six have been preserved, though not in running condition.

H-8 ALLEGHENY 2-6-6-6

Country of Origin: USA
Railway: Chesapeake & Ohio Railway (Chessie)
Date: 1941
Length Overall: 39.653m (130ft 1in)
Total Weight: 489,091kg (1,076,000lb)
Cylinders: 4 571 × 838mm (22.5 × 33in)
Driving Wheels: 1.701m (5ft 7in)
Axle Load: 39,250kg (86,350lb)
Fuel: 22,727kg (50,000lb)
Grate Area: 12.5m² (135sq ft)
Water: 94,500lit (20,800gal) (25,000 US gal)
Heating Surface: 673m² (7,240sq ft)
Superheater: 296m² (3,186sq ft)
Steam Pressure: 18.3kg/cm² (260psi)
Adhesive Weight: 214,091kg (471,000lb)
Tractive Effort: 50,000kg (110,200lb)

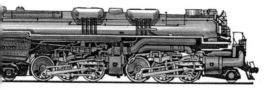

History: Two H-8 Allegheny 2-6-6-6 locomotives were capable of moving 140 coal cars weighing in total 11,500 tonnes up the climb from Hinton to the summit of the Allegheny Mountains. Built at the Lima Locomotive Works, 60 were delivered to the Chesapeake & Ohio Railway and a further 8 to the Virginian Railroad. Their working lives were very short, all of them being withdrawn in 1956 to be replaced by diesels. Though designed primarily to haul coal, the most powerful locomotives ever to be built also fitted passenger work, to which 20 were allocated at one time or another. Built of cast steel frames and with roller bearings on all axles, they also featured Baker valve gear and Worthington feed water heaters. Two have been preserved, including No. 1604 which is on exhibition at the Roanoke Transport Museum, Virginia.

CHALLENGER CLASS 4-6-6-4

Country of Origin: USA
Railway: Union Pacific Railroad (UP)
Date: 1942
Length Overall: 37.16m (121ft 11in)
Total Weight: 486,818kg (1,071,000lb)
Cylinders: 4 533 × 813mm (21 × 32in)
Driving Wheels: 1.753m (5ft 7in)
Axle Load: 30,909kg (68,000lb)
Fuel: 25,455kg (56,000lb)
Grate Area: 12.3m² (132sq ft)
Water: 94,500lit (20,800gal) (25,000 US gal)
Heating Surface: 431m² (4,642sq ft)
Superheater: 162m² (1,741sq ft)
Steam Pressure: 19.7kg/cm² (280psi)
Adhesive Weight: 184,545kg (406,000lb)
Tractive Effort: 44,100kg (97,400lb)

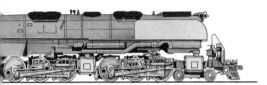

History: The claim to fame of these enormous one-million pound, articulated locomotives is that they were the largest, heaviest and the most powerful express passenger locomotives ever built. Successors to 34 freight 4-6-6-4s of 1936, which had smaller tenders, the first six were complemented by a further 65 in 1944, the latter locomotives having cast-steel frames, slightly smaller cylinders, but a higher boiler pressure. The only other major difference or improvement was the use of a vertical hinge only between the leading unit and the main frame, with the horizontal hinge being compensated for by springs on each axle. The last Challenger Class locomotive was withdrawn from service in 1958. No. 3985 has been preserved and restored to working condition at Cheyenne, Wyoming.

CLASS A-5 4-8-4

Country of Origin: USA
Railway: Northern Pacific Railroad (NP)
Date: 1943
Length Overall: 34.391m (112ft 10in)
Total Weight: 432,727kg (952,000lb)
Cylinders: 2 711 × 762mm (28 × 30in)
Driving Wheels: 1.956m (6ft 5in)
Axle Load: 33,636kg (74,000lb)
Fuel: 24,545kg (54,000lb)
Grate Area: 10.7m² (115sq ft)
Water: 95,340lit (21,000gal) (12,000 US gal)
Heating Surface: 433m² (4,660sq ft)
Superheater: 185m² (1,992sq ft)
Steam Pressure: 18.3kg/cm² (260psi)
Adhesive Weight: 13,409kg (295,000lb)
Tractive Effort: 31,660kg (69,800lb)
History: The ten Northern Pacific Railroad 4-8-4s of
1943, with their Union Pacific-type 4-10-0 tenders,
were the final descendants of a long line of A-class

4-8-4s which first entered service with NP in 1926. These original Class A locomotives were the first 4-8-4s to appear; they subsequently entered service in 1927 with the Canadian National Railway service and eventually with another 38 railroads. After NP's first 4-8-4 entered service, they never ordered another wheel combination for any passenger locomotive; instead they gradually developed the class in successive batches, until their final order for steam locomotives from Baldwin in 1943. By that time the total weight had increased by 30 per cent. They all had very large fireboxes measuring 4m × 2.5m (13ft 4in × 8ft 4in) and this enabled the creation of a world record distance of 1,608km (999mls) without an engine change from St Paul to Livingstone, Montana. There were 12 original Class A locomotives built by the American Locomotive Co (Alco). Subsequently derivatives were all built by Baldwin, 10 A-2s in 1934, 8 A-3s in 1938, 8 A-4s in 1941, and the final 10 A-5s in 1943.

CLASS UL-F 4-8-2
Country of Origin: Canada

Railway: Canadian National Railways (CNR)
Date: 1944
Length Overall: 28.426m (93ft 3in)
Total Weight: 290,000kg (638,000lb)
Cylinders: 2 610 × 762mm (24 × 30in)
Driving Wheels: 1.854mm (6ft 1in)
Axle Load: 27,045kg (59,500lb)
Fuel: 18,182kg (40,000lb)
Grate Area: 6.6m² (70.2sq ft)
Water: 52,210lit (11,500gal) (13,800 US gal)
Heating Surface: 333m² (3,584sq ft)
Superheater: 146m² (1,570sq ft)

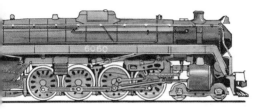

Steam Pressure: 18.3kg/cm² (260psi)
Adhesive Weight: 107,727kg (237,000lb)
Tractive Effort: 23,814kg (52,500lb)
History: Twenty 4-8-2 locomotives, designated Class ULF, were delivered to Canadian National Railways in 1934. They were descendants of a long line of UL Class eight-coupled locomotives which had first entered service in 1923. They featured cast-steel frames and exhaust steam injectors which replaced the boiler feed pump and feed water heater. Six of these handsome locomotives have been carefully preserved by CNR in operational condition.

2900 CLASS 4-8-4

Country of Origin: USA
Railway: Atchison, Topeka & Santa Fe Railway (AT&SF)
Date: 1944

Length Overall: 36.830m (120ft 10in)
Total Weight: 436,818kg (961,000lb)
Cylinders: 2 711 × 813mm (28 × 32in)
Driving Wheels: 2.032m (6ft 8in)
Axle Load: 33,636kg (74,000lb)
Fuel: 26,488lit (5,830gal) (7,000 US gal) oil
Grate Area: 10m² (108sq ft)
Water: 92,616lit (20,400gal) (24,500 US gal)
Heating Surface: 494m² (5,313sq ft)
Superheater: 220m² (2,366sq ft)
Steam Pressure: 21kg/cm² (300psi)
Adhesive Weight: 133,636kg (294,000lb)
Tractive Effort: 36,270kg (79,960lb)

History: Running on the Kansas City-Los Angeles section of the Chicago-Los Angeles main line, these 65 magnificent locomotives with their 16-wheeled fenders were scheduled to run the 2,830km (1,760mls), via the Raton Pass, without change of locomotive – the largest distances ever rostered. During the 34-hour run the crews were changed 12 times, and fuel was taken on at 12 stops and water at 16. They were the heaviest and longest straight (non-articulated) steam passenger locomotives ever built. Although none have been preserved in working condition, No. 2903 is on exhibition at the Chicago Museum of Science and Industry.

FEF-3 CLASS 4-8-4

Country of Origin: USA
Railway: Union Pacific Railroad (UP)
Date: 1944
Length Overall: 34.696m (113ft 10in)
Total Weight: 412,727kg (908,000lb)
Cylinders: 2 635 × 813mm (25 × 32in)
Driving Wheels: 2.032mm (6ft 8in)
Axle Load: 30,455kg (67,000lb)
Fuel: 22,727kg (50,000lb)
Grate Area: 9.3m² (100sq ft)
Water: 89,052lit (19,600gal) (23,500 US gal)
Heating Surface: 393m² (4,225sq ft)
Superheater: 130m² (1,400sq ft)
Steam Pressure: 21kg/cm² (300psi)
Adhesive Weight: 121,136kg (266,500lb)
Tractive Effort: 28,950kg (63,800lb)

History: Another of the single-cast cast-steel-framed locomotives, the FEF-3 also boasted a static exhaust steam injector to drive the water pump and feed the water heater. More revolutionary, however, was the introduction of highly successful coupling rods for the main motion; these were forked at each end and connected to the wheels by separate sleeve bearings instead of through crankpins, thus dispensing with the knuckling joints in the rods. The first of the class appeared in 1938, designated FEF-1; they numbered 20 and had 12-wheeled tenders. Fifteen FEF-2s appeared in 1939, identical to the final 10 locomotives of 1944, designated FEF-3. After World War II they were converted to oil burning and were withdrawn from service by 1959. No. 814 (an FEF-1) is preserved at Dodge Park, Council Bluffs, Omaha.

NIAGARA CLASS 4-8-4

Country of Origin: USA
Railway: New York Central Railroad (NYC)
Date: 1945
Length Overall: 35.192m (115ft 5.5in)
Total Weight: 405,000kg (891,000lb)
Cylinders: 2 648 × 813mm (25.5 × 32in)
Driving Wheels: 2.007m (6ft 7in)
Axle Load: 31,818kg (70,000lb)
Fuel: 41,818kg (92,000lb)
Grate Area: 9.3m² (100sq ft)
Water: 68,100lit (15,000gal) (18,000 US gal)
Heating Surface: 4.48m² (4,827sq ft)
Superheater: 191m² (2,060sq ft)
Steam Pressure: 19.3kg/cm² (275psi)
Adhesive Weight: 124,545kg (274,000lb)
Tractive Effort: 27,936kg (61,570lb)

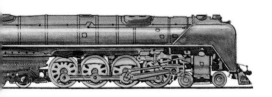

History: Built by the American Locomotive Company, the Niagara Class 4-8-4s were not too dissimilar to the FEF-2 Class being operated by the Union Pacific Railroad. Baker's valve gear replaced Walschaert's and the smokestack was virtually non-existent due to the height limit of 4.62m (15ft 2in) of the NYC. By 1945 standard American building practices meant an integral cast-steel frame and axles and coupling rods with roller bearings. Twenty-five locomotives were built, plus a prototype and an experimental poppet-valve version. They were designed to run the 12 daily trains between New York and Chicago with just one coaling stop. This service included the famous Twentieth Century Limited, which made the journey in just 16 hours, taking on water with a pick-up scoop at 128km/h (80mph).

141R LIBERATION 2-8-2

Country of Origin: France

Railway: French National Railways (SNCF)
Date: 1945
Length Overall: 26.161m (79ft 3in)
Total Weight: 18,809kg (413,800lb)
Cylinders: 2 596 × 711mm (23.5 × 28in)
Driving Wheels: 1.65m (5ft 5in)
Axle Load: 22,050kg (48,510lb)
Fuel: 10,909kg (24,000lb)
Grate Area: 5.2m² (55.5sq ft)
Water: 1,468lit (6,666gal) (8,000 US gal)
Heating Surface: 251m² (2,699sq ft)
Superheater: 65m² (704sq ft)
Steam Pressure: 1.4kg/cm² (20psi)
Adhesive Weight: 80,182kg (176,400lb)
Tractive Effort: 20,191kg (44,500lb)

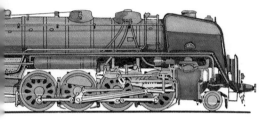

History: An incredible 1,340 Class 141R locomotives were ordered by SNCF from North America after World War II to replace those destroyed. Built by Alco, Baldwin, Lima, the Montreal Loco Works and the Canadian Loco Co., the locomotives were all delivered between 1945 and 1947. Minor improvements and alterations were continually made, including the introduction of cast steel beds with integral cylinders, roller bearings and Boxpok wheels to replace the spoked ones. Many of the later locomotives were delivered as oil burners and some were converted in France to help combat severe coal shortages. The engines proved to be both successful and economical and they were the last steam locomotives in service with SNCF.

WEST COUNTRY CLASS 4-6-2

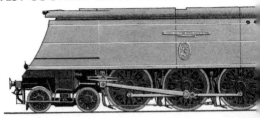

Country of Origin: Great Britain
Railway: Southern Railway (SR)
Date: 1946
Length Overall: 20.542m (67ft 4.75in)
Total Weight: 138,182kg (304,000lb)
Cylinders: 3 416 × 610mm (16.7 × 24in)
Driving Wheels: 1.879m (6ft 2in)
Axle Load: 20,227kg (44,500lb)
Fuel: 5,000kg (11,000lb)
Grate Area: 3.55m² (38.25sq ft)
Water: 24,970lit (5,500gal) (6,600 US gal)
Heating Surface: 197m² (2,122sq ft)
Superheater: 50.6m² (545sq ft)
Steam Pressure: 19.7kg/cm² (280psi)
Adhesive Weight: 59,545kg (131,000lb)
Tractive Effort: 14,083kg (31,046lb)
History: The first of 140 4-6-2 locomotives, the 31
Merchant Navy Class (which included a prototype of
1941) were followed by the 109-strong, slightly

smaller West Country Class which first appeared in 1945 and included what became known as the Battle of Britain Class. All except six were built at Southern Railways' Brighton Works and featured welded boilers, steel fireboxes, and patent chain-driven valve gear placed inside an oil-filled sump positioned between the frames. Unhappily, the West Country Class locomotives were not a success, being expensive to both build and run; in addition, their sumps leaked and continually broke, and they were very prone to wheel slip. Designed by SR's Chief Mechanical Engineer, Oliver Bulleid, the West Country Class were used throughout SR's system, including hauling the Golden Arrow train from London Victoria to Dover Docks. Many were immeasurably improved in 1960, with new cylinders and motion. They remained in service until the very last days of steam in Britain in 1967.

242 A1 4-8-4

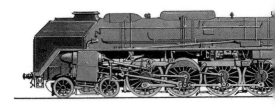

Country of Origin: France
Railway: French National Railways (SNCF)
Date: 1946
Length Overall: 17.765m (58ft 3.5in)
Total Weight: 225,455kg (496,000lb)
Cylinders: HP: 1 600 × 720mm (23.6 × 28.3in); LP: 2 680 × 760mm (27 × 29.9in)
Driving Wheels: 1.95m (6ft 4.75in)
Axle Load: 21,136kg (46,500lb)
Fuel: 11,364kg (25,000lb)
Grate Area: 5m² (54sq ft)
Water: 34,050lit (7,500gal) (9,000 US gal)
Heating Surface: 253m² (2,720sq ft)
Superheater: 120m² (1,249sq ft)
Steam Pressure: 20.4kg/cm² (290psi)
Adhesive Weight: 84,318kg (185,500lb)

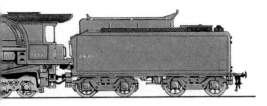

History: The first locomotive to be built in France after World War II, the 2-4-2 A1 Class was also France's first 4-8-4. They had a high-pressure cylinder inside, which drove the leading main axle, and two low-pressure cylinders outside, driving the second axle. Designed by the remarkable locomotive engineer André Chapelon, other features included double piston-valves, two thermic syphons in the firebox, a mechanical stoker, and a triple Kylchap chimney. Chapelon's masterpiece was a one-off, the most powerful locomotive outside North America; it was a match for any diesel or electric locomotive, and was also extremely fuel efficient. Unfortunately it came at a time when the French government was determined to electrify, and this marvellous example of steam locomotion was quietly withdrawn and broken up.

CLASS A1 4-6-2

Country of Origin: Great Britain
Railway: British Railways (BR)

Date: 1948
Length Overall: 22.25m (73ft)
Total Weight: 167,727kg (369,000lb)
Cylinders: 3 482 × 660mm (19 × 26in)
Driving Wheels: 2.032m (6ft 8in)
Axle Load: 22,500kg (49,500lb)
Fuel: 9,091kg (20,000lb)
Grate Area: 4.6m² (50sq ft)
Water: 22,700lit (5,000gal) (6,000 US gal)
Heating Surface: 228.6m² (2,461sq ft)
Superheater: 63.2m² (680sq ft)
Steam Pressure: 17.6kg/cm² (250psi)
Adhesive Weight: 67,273kg (148,000lb)
Tractive Effort: 16,900kg (37,400lb)

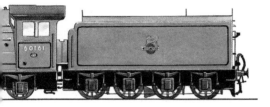

History: Fast, economical locomotives, the Class A1s recorded a daily average of 325km (202mls) over a period of 12 years. The 49 engines required little maintenance and some remained in service until the last days of British main-line steam. After World War II a rebuilding programme was embarked upon by Gresley's successor, Edward Thompson, but the full extent of rebuilding improvements and refinements only made any impact after Arthur Peppercorn (who had become Thompson's assistant with the full cooperation of the Doncaster drawing office), quietly embarked upon further modifications, from which 15 Class A2 locomotives evolved prior to the emergence of the very successful A1s.

CLASS 241P 4-8-2

Country of Origin: France
Railway: French National Railways (SNCF)
Date: 1948
Length Overall: 27.418m (89ft 11in)

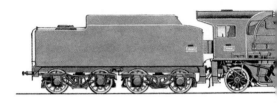

Total Weight: 214,545kg (472,000lb)
Cylinders: HP: 2 446 × 650mm (17.6 × 25.6in); LP: 2 674 × 700mm (26.5 × 27.6in)
Driving Wheels: 2.01m (6ft 7.1in)
Axle Load: 20,455kg (45,000lb)
Fuel: 10,000kg (22,000lb)
Grate Area: 5.1m² (54.4sq ft)
Water: 33,959lit (7,480gal) (8,980 US gal)
Heating Surface: 244.6m² (2,633sq ft)
Superheater: 108m² (1,163sq ft)
Steam Pressure: 20kg/cm² (284psi)
Adhesive Weight: 82,227kg (180,900lb)

History: The Class was based on a 1930s PLM 4-8-2, with high-pressure cylinders inside the frame driving the third axle, and low-pressure cylinders outside, driving the second axle. Many of Chapelon's innovations were incorporated to improve the performance of the superheaters. In addition a feed water heater and a mechanical stoker were added. Production of the 35 locomotives was slow and their performance not spectacular, but they were worked mercilessly for 20 years until finally replaced by diesels in 1968. No. 241P16 is in exhibition at the French National Railway Museum, Mulhouse.

C62 CLASS 4-6-4

Country of Origin: Japan
Railway: Japanese National Railways (JNR)
Date: 1949
Length Overall: 21.475m (70ft .5in)

Total Weight: 161,818kg (356,000lb)
Cylinders: 2 521 × 660mm (20.5× 26in)
Driving Wheels: 1.75m (5ft 9in)
Axle Load: 16,591kg (36,500lb)
Fuel: 10,000kg (22,000lb)
Grate Area: 3.85m² (41.5sq ft)
Water: 22,019lit (4,850gal) (5,820 US gal)
Heating Surface: 245m² (2,640sq ft) including superheater
Steam Pressure: 16kg/cm² (228psi)
Adhesive Weight: 64,773kg (142,500lb)
Tractive Effort: 13,925kg (30,690lb)

History: The most impressive of Japanese steam locomotives, the C62 Class 'Swallows' were the result of an extensive rebuilding programme of D52 Mikados, which had been built during World War II. The C62s incorporated a feed water heater with a steam pump, and an electric light. Japanese steam locomotives had always followed an American pattern ever since they purchased their first engines from Baldwin at the turn of the century, with the size scaled down to suit the 1.067m (3ft 6in) gauge. The C62 Class 4-6-4s were employed on all main-line express trains, and two have been preserved.

CLASS YP 4-6-2

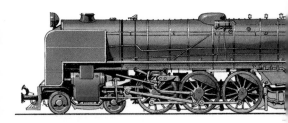

Country of Origin: India
Railway: Indian Railways (IR)
Date: 1949
Length Overall: 19.088m (62ft 7.5in)
Total Weight: 99,318kg (218,500lb)
Cylinders: 2 387 × 610mm (15.25 × 24in)
Driving Wheels: 1.372m (4ft 6in)
Axle Load: 10,682kg (23,500lb)
Fuel: 9,773kg (21,500lb)
Grate Area: 2.6m² (28sq ft)
Water: 13,620lit (3,000gal) (3,600 US gal)
Heating Surface: 103m² (1,112sq ft)
Superheater: 31m² (331sq ft)
Steam Pressure: 14.8kg/cm² (210psi)
Adhesive Weight: 31,364kg (69,000lb)

Tractive Effort: 8,731kg (18,450lb)

History: Production of the YP 4-6-2s ceased in 1970, the last passenger steam locomotives to be built anywhere in the world. Some 871 were produced and today nearly all of them remain in service, despite the gradual introduction of diesels. The Indian network being partly a metre (3ft 4in) gauge system, the Indian Railways locomotives (like those of Japan) tended to be scaled-down versions of American Baldwin engines, and the 20 prototype locomotives were supplied by Baldwin. The main production locomotives were produced at Jamshedpur by the Tata Engineering and Locomotive Company of India, but the North British Locomotive Co. of Glasgow and Krauss-Maffei of Munich also produced 300 between them.

CLASS 11 4-8-2

Country of Origin: Angola
Railway: Benguela Railway (FCB)
Date: 1951
Length Overall: 21.107m (69ft 3in)
Total Weight: 134,091kg (295,000lb)

Cylinders: 2 533 × 660mm (21 × 26in)
Driving Wheels: 1.372m (4ft 6in)
Axle Load: 13,182kg (29,000lb)
Fuel: 18.5m³ (650cu ft) wood
Grate Area: 3.7m² (40sq ft)
Water: 22,700lit (5,000gal) (6,000 US gal)
Heating Surface: 165m² (1,777sq ft)
Superheater: 39m² (420sq ft)
Steam Pressure: 14.1kg/cm² (200psi)
Adhesive Weight: 52,727kg (116,000lb)

Tractive Effort: 16,375kg (36,025lb)

History: Built by the North British Locomotive Company of Glasgow to a specification that required the engines to be able to haul 500 tonnes up 1-in-80 gradients, and to have axle loads not exceeding 13 tonnes, the six Class 11 locomotives also featured a steam-operated fire door, electric lights, a recording speedometer, and a Kylchap exhaust system. A cage was fitted to the top of the tender to hold the timber. Used primarily for hauling copper trains, the engines were kept in very good condition and have recently been converted to oil burning.

CLASS 8 4-6-2

Country of Origin: Great Britain
Railway: British Railways (BR)

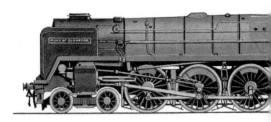

Date: 1953
Length Overall: 21.336m (70ft)
Total Weight: 157,727kg (347,000lb)
Cylinders: 3 457 × 711mm (18 × 28in)
Driving Wheels: 1.88m (6ft 2in)
Axle Load: 22,500kg (49,500lb)
Fuel: 10,000kg (22,000lb)
Grate Area: 4.5m² (48.5sq ft)
Water: 19,635lit (4,325gal) (5,200 US gal)
Heating Surface: 231m² (2,490sq ft)
Superheater: 64m² (691sq ft)
Steam Pressure: 17.6kg/cm² (250psi)
Adhesive Weight: 67,273kg (148,000lb)
Tractive Effort: 17,731kg (39,080lb)

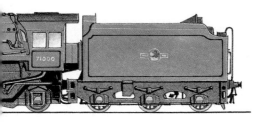

History: The *Duke of Gloucester* Class 8 4-6-2 was in fact only a prototype, and no Class 8 production locomotives were ever built. Designed as an express passenger locomotive, testing proved satisfactory, with the amount of steam used for work done creating a world record for its type. However, there were problems with the design, and unfortunately it was decided that 1953 was too late for further steam-traction development and the *Duke of Gloucester* was scrapped. The Class 8 had been immediately preceded by 55 Class 7 Britannia 4-6-2 locomotives, which were used extensively throughout the British Railways system and proved to be both economical and efficient.

CLASS 25 4-8-4

Country of Origin: South Africa
Railway: South African Railways (SAR)
Date: 1953
Length Overall: 32.772m (107ft 6.25in)
Total Weight: 238,636kg (525,000lb)
Cylinders: 2 610 × 711mm (24 × 28in)
Driving Wheels: 1.524m (5ft)
Axle Load: 20,000kg (44,000lb)
Fuel: 19,091kg (42,000lb)
Grate Area: 6.5m² (70sq ft)
Water: 19,976lit (4,400gal) (5,300 US gal)
Heating Surface: 315m² (3,390sq ft)
Superheater: 58.5m² (630sq ft)
Steam Pressure: 15.8kg/cm² (225psi)
Adhesive Weight: 78,182kg (172,000lb)
Tractive Effort: 20,578kg (45,360lb)

History: The Class 25 4-8-4s are the only condensing locomotives to be featured in this book. The 90 that were built came about as a direct result of the necessity to overcome the enormous cost involved in transporting water to stations across the Karoo Desert. Experiments with a condensing locomotive built by Henschel in Germany showed a saving of 90 per cent of the water normally used, in addition to a 10 per cent saving on coal; the condenser was fitted to a very long tender. Production orders were placed with North British Locomotive Co. The engines featured roller bearings, and a one-piece frame which included the cylinders and a very large boiler. Only one of these fascinating locomotives has been preserved in working condition, and it is still able to demonstrate the total lack of puff normally associated with the starting of any steam locomotive.

CLASS 59 4-8-2 + 2-8-4

Country of Origin: Kenya
Railway: East African Railways (EAR)

Date: 1955
Length Overall: 31.737m (104ft 1.5in)
Total Weight: 256,364kg (564,000lb)
Cylinders: 4 521 × 711mm (20.5 × 28in)
Driving Wheels: 1.372m (4ft 6in)
Axle Load: 21,364kg (47,000lb)
Fuel: 12,267lit (2,700gal) (3,250 US gal) oil
Grate Area: 6.7m² (72sq ft)
Water: 39,044lit (8,600gal) (10,400 US gal)
Heating Surface: 331m² (3,560sq ft)
Superheater: 69.4m² (747sq ft)
Steam Pressure: 15.8kg/cm² (225psi)
Adhesive Weight: 162,273kg (357,000lb)
Tractive Effort: 38,034kg (83,350lb)

History: Thirty-four of these huge Garrett Class 59 locomotives were built by Beyer, Peacock of Manchester, with the express purpose of hauling freight, of which an unprecedented backlog had accumulated for shipment by East African Railways. The engines were built to be easily converted from the metre (3ft 4in) gauge of the Kenya and Ugandan Railways to the 1.067m (3ft 6in) African standard gauge. They also had a mechanical stoker so that they could be converted from oil to coal burning if required. The Class 59s were eventually replaced by diesels, with the last being withdrawn from service in 1980, but not before they had had their day as the world's largest and most powerful steam locomotives.

Index